Shadow of the Other

Shadow of the Other

Intersubjectivity and Gender
in Psychoanalysis

Jessica Benjamin

Routledge
Taylor & Francis Group
New York   London

Routledge

711 Third Avenue, New York, NY 10017

Published in Great Britain by

Routledge

2 Park Square, Milton Park, Abingdon, Oxon OX14 4RN

Copyright © 1998 by Routledge

Library of Congress Cataloging-in-Publication Data

Benjamin, Jessica.
    Shadow of the other : intersubjectivity and gender in
    psychoanalysis / Jessica Benjamin.
        p.   cm.
    Includes bibliographical references and index.
    ISBN 0-415-91236-9 (hardcover). — ISBN 0-415-91237-7 (pbk.)
    1. Psychoanalysis and feminism.   I. Title
    BF175.4.F45B45   1998
    150.19´5´082—dc21   98-14660

This book is dedicated with love to my friends—travelling companions through the great changes of the last three decades—they didn't all work out as we hoped, but they have been amazing changes all the same.

Contents

Acknowledgments

I wish to thank all my patients, my students (especially Monday morning), and colleagues (at NYU Postdoc and Psybc. com) with and from whom I have learned so much over the years. My gratitude also to Lewis Aron, Fran Bartkowski, Teresa Brennan, Donna Bassin, Muriel Dimen, Virginia Goldner, Dan Hill, and Zina Steinberg, who have contributed, with comments, ideas and encouragement, to my thinking and working on these essays. To my children, Jonah and Jake, who have been an ever-present source of affirmation, hope, and necessary distraction, and to Andy, who has made so much possible, I am most grateful.

Introduction

In 1979, while I was engaged in organizing a large conference on feminist theory to commemorate "The Second Sex—Thirty Years Later," I had the opportunity to meet with and interview Simone de Beauvoir. Recently, my co-interviewer, Margaret Simons, asked me how it was that when she had become discouraged in her efforts to gain ackowledgement from de Beauvoir that she herself was the origin of some of her own and Sartre's most profound philosophical ideas, I leaned forward and asked de Beauvoir, "So when you wrote in *She Came to Stay* that Francoise says what really upsets her about Xaviere is that she has to confront in her another consciousness, that is not an idea that particularly came from Sartre?" To which de Beauvoir replied, "It was I who thought about that! It was absolutely not Sartre." I persisted, "But that is an idea which it seems to me appears later in his work," and de Beauvoir replied "Oh! Maybe! In any case, this problem of the other's consciousness, it was my problem." (Simons & Benjamin, 1979; Simons in press) The answer to Simons' question was, of course, that I recognized this problem, for it has preoccupied me as well. I had underlined it the moment I came across it in the novel, and noted when it was written.

The problem of how we relate to the fact of the other's independent consciousness, a mind that is fundamentally like our own but unfathomably different and outside our control, has been a through line in my work. At the time of that interview, I was writing about it in relation to Hegel's understanding of the master-slave dialectic and the depiction of sadomasochism in the *Story of O*. This dialectical encounter of two consciousnesses became the basis for my understanding of intersubjectivity in *The Bonds of Love* (Benjamin, 1988) and later in *Like Subjects, Love Objects* (Benjamin, 1995). The essence of the intersubjective perspective is, "where objects were, subjects must be." Freud's insight that "the shadow of the object fell upon the ego" unveiled the process of identification. Understanding the shadow cast by the other in the space in-between seems to me an apt metaphor for intersubjectivity.

In these essays I take up once again the interface between intersubjectivity and gender. My aim, as in the past, is to work in the space defined by the overlapping concerns of psychoanalysis and feminist theory. This book is more focused than previous ones on issues raised by postmodern approaches in contemporary theory that emphasize the problem of difference, the subject's position, and the construction of knowledge. However, I continue to conceptualize the problems central to psychoanalysis in terms of the double task of recognition: how both analyst and patient make known their own subjectivity and recognize the other's. In current relational analysis we see a reversal that restores the analyst's subjectivity as a fallible being and the analysand's subjectivity as one who can know and speak with authority. My intention is to push beyond this reversal by contemplating the difficulty of creating or discovering the space in which it is possible for either subject to recognize the difference of the other.

The practical and theoretical possibilities that the contemporary focus on intersubjectivity has opened up are truly exciting and, although not discussed clinically in great detail, they have been the backdrop for this book. My effort has been to address underlying issues that I consider fundamental to the intersubjective perspective as a whole. (Some of them, especially in the third essay, may seem highly theoretical to those who are primarily interested in the clinical experience of intersubjectivity. Some readers might find it easier to begin with the second essay in which I give some of the theoretical background.) This effort is inspired by the belief that the clinical experiences opened up by the discussion of intersubjectivity deserve to be raised to the level of theory where they will have an impact on other kinds of theorizing, which, too often, have relied on Freud alone for their psychoanalytic perspective. This is not to say that in my view the "classical" intrapsychic viewpoint is no longer of value—on the contrary, I continue to strongly believe that the intrapsychic and intersubjective views cannot replace or dispense with one another, and draw much of their meaning from the contrast between them. But I do think that the ongoing discussion about intersubjectivity in psychoanalysis should have a chance to inform contemporary theory outside psychoanalysis in a much deeper way than it has done so far. This book aims to bring the psychoanalytic discussion into a context for those interested in feminist and critical theory, as well as to bring their broader theoretical concerns into psychoanalysis.

In this book I continue to elaborate my perspective on the double task of recognition in psychoanalysis. Central to this task as I define it is the matter of how we use our marvelous capacity for identification with others to either further or impede our recognition of others, to bridge or obfuscate differences between us. Or rather, I am concerned with how we do both at once. These two sides of identification often seem to present a choice, which leads to a parting of the ways in psychoanalysis. We might note two distinct tendencies, each emphasizing one side of identification. There are those psychoanalytic thinkers, notably Lacan and Fairbairn, who, though quite different, see the tendency to incorporate the other as a mental object primarily in its defensive, "cannibalistic" (Grotstein, in conversation) and imaginary aspects, that is, as inimical to recognizing difference. Then again, proponents of Kleinian analysis, American ego psychology, or self psychology stress, each in their own way, the structure-building or functional aspects of identification or introjection. As is my usual tendency, I am inclined to see the merit of both viewpoints, and to try to work with the tension between them. On the one hand, I think it important to see the creative use that the mind makes of the identifications it inevitably develops. On the other, I emphasize the intersubjective relationship in which one goes beyond identification to appreciate the other subject as a being outside the self. Thus I try to elaborate the distinction between kinds of identification: those that can help break up an apparent objectivity based on distance, and those that simply draw us into a see-saw relationship (see Lacan, 1988) in which we can no longer perceive the other.

The structure of complementarity, the see-saw in which we can incessantly reverse positions through identification, is fundamental to our intrapsychic understanding of mind. The essays in this book explore a series of complementary structures and familiar polarities, showing how we move in and out of entanglement in them. Subject and object, active and passive, observer and participant, knower and known—these reversible complementarities have structured the psychoanalytic relationship. The intersubjective perspective is concerned with how we create the third position that is able to break up the reversible complementarities and hold in tension the polarities that underly them. Essential to that theoretical aim is the uncovering of the gender coding of these complementarities, which has so successfully inscribed them in our desire, in our psyches.

In the first essay in this book, I discuss the early history of Freud's work on hysteria—his discovery of psychoanalysis, its origin (in German *Ursprung,* meaning literally "primal leap"). Here we can see the first complementary form that structured the psychoanalytic endeavor, that between knowing subject and object of knowledge. I show how this structure tended to undermine the aim of the psychoanalytic project, which was to bring the inarticulate subject to speech—a project shared by psychoanalysis and femininism. Inspired by the trajectory of Anna O. from "first" patient to founding feminist and beginning with Freud's discussions of hysteria, I consider how the analyst's sense of her or his relation to the patient has evolved. While this essay is written from the perspective of our journey as analysts, it is about coming closer to the subjective experience of the patient through the acknowledgement of our not-so-different subjectivity. In short, I try to show how the position of the analyst is affected by the identification with the patient, and how the analytic stance has changed in accord with that recognition.

These reflections have been inspired by the recent efforts to break down the objectivism prescribed by Freud, which, even in our time, so deeply suffused the analytic enterprise (Gill, 1994). The opposition between analyst as knowing subject and analysand as known object assumed the analyst's distance from a disenfranchised other. The objectivist stance, which disowned the analyst's subjectivity, necessarily brought about impasses and contradictions because the inevitable return of the repressed—the analyst's identification with the analysand—appeared as a dangerous breakdown of the analytic posture rather than a necessary, potentially creative, part of the endeavor. Reconfiguring the analytic relationship toward subjectivity has a double meaning: both recognizing the subjectivity of the analyst and elevating the patient to the position of a subject who collaborates and knows. The move out of the subject-object complementarity, in which the subject who observes disavows his own participation, also helps to overcome the objectivist split between observation and participation (see Aron, 1995). The intersubjective view of psychoanalysis not only needs to postulate that the analyst is a participant, but also to conceive of a third position of true observation. This third position is founded in the communicative relationship, which creates a dialogue that is an entity in itself, a potential space outside the web of identifications. (Ogden, 1994 posits the analytic dialogue as a "third," but my meaning here is limited to an internal mental space created through a dialogue that recognizes the other.) Through the space created by two subjectivities we can observe even as we repeat the incessant reversal of opposites, the see-saw relations that are brought about through our identification with the object.

It is my view that the reintegration of subjectivity and mutuality in the analytic relationship should be seen as part of a larger intersubjective project to which feminism has contributed as much as psychoanalysis. I think this because only the re-presentation of the mother in contemporary analytic thought has allowed the intersubjective perspective to emerge. The idea that self-other dialogue is the fundamental basis for the development of mind (Stern, 1985; Spezzano, 1996a) has evolved in tandem with our revaluing of the early maternal dyad, its affective and communicative possibilities. In the classical psychoanalytic emphasis on the father, the mother's work in maintaining and producing life was taken for granted, rather than represented, and so the alienation of the subject from that which created and maintained "his" life was reproduced. In psychoanalytic terms, maternal work is above all that of representing, reflecting and containing the child's mind— which is also the basic work of the analyst. Let us briefly consider the implications of the fact that the mother's mental work is so essential to the constitution of mind, and yet the mother's own subjectivity was not represented.

Kojeve (1969), in discussing Hegel's master-slave dialectic, shows how the slave did the work that mediated the master's enjoyment of the object, without having enjoyment himself, while the master, who had enjoyment, had no direct contact with the object of desire. Thus the two aspects of subjectivity—transforming the object and enjoying the desire for it—were split, and neither subject could own their desire. To transpose this psychoanalytically: only when the mother has her own enjoyment as a subject of desire, and when the (formerly) male subject does his own mental work of representing and holding desire, is this split overcome—creating the third position. Intersubjectivity thus requires that each subject own and enjoy her or his own desire as well as the activity which realizes it.

This intersubjective recasting of the relation of desire also destabilizes the active-passive dichotomy, which was so central to Freud's understanding of masculinity and femininity. This theme is not only important to my discussion of how the analyst-patient dyad can change, but also to the discussion of gender in the second essay. Here, again, I try to expose some of the contradictions and impasses that have resulted from the complementarities of subject and object, active and passive. I do this, in part, by analyzing the conflict that appeared in feminist psychoanalytic thought in the last two decades regarding Freud: the conflict between the Lacanian view (Mitchell, 1982; Rose, 1982), which follows Freud, and the object relations view (Chodorow, 1978), which critiqued Freud. Put somewhat simply, while the Lacanian view takes the phallus or father as starting point, the object relations view takes the mother. For the adherents of Freud, masculinity is presumed and femininity defined as its other; for the revisionists, maternal identification is primary and masculinity comes into being as not-mother. By juxtaposing the two sides of the argument, I show that the "truth" of each position leads us to the ambiguity of gender: masculinity and femininity can each be construed as the negation of the other—its opposite, its complementary other. This confirms the view shared by myself and other relational thinkers that gender as we now know it works through a mutual and symmetrical determination of opposing terms, which can shift in tandem, rather than through essential, fixed qualities (Dimen, 1991; Harris, 1991; Goldner, 1991).

However, this ambiguity and lack of definite content is only part of the story. For it is also readily evident that patriarchal culture has historically given certain contents to these gender categories. Thus Freud's description of femininity may be taken as a real appearance within patriarchal culture, whose recognizable content may be traced to a specific psychic constellation. This constellation, I propose, is actually the boy's oedipal posture in which the identification with mother is repudiated, and the elements of passivity associated with his own babyhood are projected onto the girl, the daughter. This projection determines the daughter's position as that of passive container for the male's defensively organized activity. Accepting this "feminine passivity" in her oedipal turn to the father, the daughter's position, upon which Freud and his followers so vehemently insisted, does appear to constitute the content of femininity as we know it. Activity and passivity are thus divided in the oedipal position, foreclosing the possibility of being a subject who would own both tendencies within the self.

Yet, I contend, this split is endemic only to the oedipal constellation, with its emphasis on the mutual exclusivity of each gender's position and the repudiation of the opposite sex identifications. The overcoming of the defensive splitting that characterizes the oedipal complementarity of masculinity and femininity is not as difficult to conceive as previous psychoanalytic theory presumed. By recapturing the bisexual identifications of the preoedipal position, we counterbalance the oedipal postion of mutual exclusivity in which we can only be like the one or the other. This recuperation of earlier bisexuality in the postoedipal complementarity challenges the apparent immutability of the polarities activity and passivity, masculinity and femininity.

Here I propose that authorship, or ownership, of our desire and intention is a crucial feature of subjectivity occluded by the conventional opposition between activity and passivity. As in my earlier discussion of "a desire of one's own," (Benjamin 1986b, 1988) I show how being a subject of desire requires ownership and not merely activity. Ownership depends upon reclaiming the maternal form of activity, the recognition and holding of emotional states, excitement in particular. While we use the patrocentric theory to understand the form conventionally assumed by femininity (see Brennen, 1992), we use the matrocentric theory to formulate the mother's contribution to our subjectivity and desire.

In a rather different way the question of recuperating what has been disowned informs my final exploration in the third essay of subjectivity and otherness, which deals most directly with the problem of recognition. Here I propose that the philosophical questioning of the subject, which has been an important issue in recent feminist theory, needs to be put in relation to the idea of the self, which is not reducible to the philosophical subject. This essay was partly inspired by a need to clarify my position in response to the reception of my theory of recognition in feminist theory.[1] My effort to set up a critique of the splitting between assertion and recognition, separation and connection, has often been read as a one-sided defense of one aspect, usually of connection or recognition against separation and assertion of subjectivity (see Weir, 1996; Meyers 1994; Scott, 1993). Actually, I contended that the problem lies in splitting, the breakdown of tension between these tendencies—in other words, that breakdown can lead to one-sided adherence to either side of the polarity. It is true that I emphasized the aspect of domination that arises from the masculine position of hyper-individuation, but that posture is obviously the flip side of feminine submission. After all, in relationships based on splitting, one term reciprocally determines the other. Weir, however, argues that I sacrifice the concept of autonomy in favor of recognition, defined only as affective attunement, and that I see separation as inevitably sliding into domination. Indeed, I consider affective recognition to be central in infancy, but it is followed by confrontation with the tension between assertion and recognition: the clash of independent wills, the negotiation of conflict beginning in rapprochement in the second year of life. Regarding this phase, I emphasize girls' and boys' need for a father who represents separate subjectivity and desire for the outside world. The idea of recognition, as I understand it, has to contain within it the aspect of the assertion of separate subjectivity—else there is nothing to recognize.

In addition, my argument that the splitting of antithetical psychic tendencies underlies domination has been read as the simple proposition that separation and connection must remain in balance (Benhabib, 1992a; Butler, 1990b). My sense is that the conclusion of *The Bonds of Love*—in which I stressed the necessary process wherein recognition breaks down and must be restored—either came too late or was insufficiently compelling. In any event, this essay aims to rectify that problem by clarifying that in the dialectic between recognition and negation the negating aspect is equally crucial.

This negating moment is decisive for the problem of accepting difference and otherness. Since the different other is a threat to the identity of the self or ego that wants to be all there is, that wants to

---

[1] Discussing recognition on a philosophical level, Meyers (1994) has argued for a notion of self-recognition as indispensable to the kind of mutuality I am proposing. I think she is correct, and that such self-recognition is part of the evolution of what I am calling authorship or ownership.

assimilate everything into itself, much critical theory and philosophy have addressed the problem of identity. In this essay I aim to show how the intersubjective relation can keep alive the negative moment while maintaining the possibility for recognition. My point of departure is Winnicott's radical rethinking of how otherness can be accepted by the self when the attempt to psychically destroy the object is resolved through the other's survival. I have elaborated this idea by proposing that a symmetry is necessary in which both self and other must own the burden of subjectivity, the tendency to assimilate or deny the difference of the other (destruction). We must not only recognize our tendency to destroy, we must survive for the other; and we must also ask the other to take on the onus of being a subject and surviving our destruction. In reaching this idea, I have drawn on the clinical experience of guilt and acquiescence to the other's narcissism to forestall being in the destructive position. At the same time I am stressing the social implications of realizing that the onus of subjectivity must be borne even by those cast in the position of other, for they aspire to the subject position as well.

It may be that in emphasizing this common burden of subjectivity, as well as in my overall belief in the possibility of mutual recognition that survives negation, I lean toward one side of the tension between difference and commonality. That is, if the choice is between the idea that in facing the problem of recognition we are all struggling with common human difficulties, or the idea that we can never know the other and our effort to do so is apt to abrogate respect for difference, I lean toward the former. Since the process of thinking inevitably requires movement through opposition, there is always the matter of whether we will strive to incorporate or repel different ideas. I readily acknowledge that I am inclined toward incorporation, synthesis of opposing ideas. It is my suspicion that no matter how self-conscious we try to be about these choices, everyone leans in one direction or other. Presumably, one's own tendency to lean will always inspire some opposite movement, some negation by others, that pushes our thought further—leaving our psyches scrambling to catch up.

I hope that my moves through the field of psychoanalysis—engaging in all the mental work of incorporating and critiquing, linking and opposing thoughts—will partake in and invite some creative interplay of negation and recognition by others. The inevitable limits of my perspective will, I trust, be revealed in dialogue with others that can stimulate new possibilities. In such engagement with others whose horizons are different there is always, as Spezzano (1996) points out, the "risk of being transformed." This risk reflects the reciprocity of dialogue, the inevitable fact that the other will share our wish to affect, have impact on, tranform others. Challenging identity always threatens to be a reciprocal process, and in psychoanalysis our "subject" can always surprise us, turn the tables on us, transform us, painful as that may be. In the past, rigidity and orthodoxy often prevented theoretical dialogue from living up to and deepening the collaborative commitment to transformation. It created a mode of training and practice in which gravity suppressed play and authority stifled collaboration. The current climate of discussion and debate in psychoanalysis gives reason to hope that we may enlarge the dialogic space that engenders the third position, that the oppositions we present can play in freedom their hour upon the stage.

1

The Primal Leap* of Psychoanalysis, From Body to Speech

Freud, Feminism, and the Vicissitudes of the Transference

I

In reflecting on the one-hundredth anniversary of *Studies on Hysteria*, I felt impelled to remember an earlier point, the seventy-fifth anniversary, in which the rebirth of the feminist movement occurred—a movement that had at least equal importance for the inventor of the "talking cure," Anna O., a movement that has been shadowing psychoanalysis since its inception and has, in our time, called for and led to a massive revision in how we view ourselves and the subjects of those original *Studies*. Without the additional surge of the feminist movement, I would not be here as a psychoanalyst today, nor would I be able to say what I have to say. So it seemed worth noting the coincidence that, on the occasion of the seventy-fifth anniversary of psychoanalysis, I was, without realizing it, living just around the corner from the Leerbachstrasse in Frankfurt, where

---

* Origins = *Ur Sprung* in German, literally "primal leap." This paper was originally delivered in May, 1995 at a conference commemorating the hundredth anniversary of the *Studies*, "The Psychoanalytic Century," at NYU. Thanks to M. Dimen and A. Harris.

1

Anna O., known to her world as Bertha Pappenheim, settled after her recovery from hysterical illness in the 1890's.

Anna O. was the patient of Freud's older colleague Breuer, coauthor of *Studies on Hysteria*, and it was her treatment on which Freud based the connection between hysterical symptoms and specific ideas or feelings that could not be otherwise expressed. It was also her intense attachment to Breuer that led to a precipitous end to the treatment by the frightened physician and so inspired the founding myth of transference love as Freud conveyed it to us.[1]

Frankfurt was not an accidental choice, in the 1890s or the 1960s. As an historically independent, liberal city and center of finance, the site of the 1848 democratic parliament, Frankfurt was home to an important Jewish bourgeoisie before the Third Reich and was the center of "Red Hessen"'s social democratic movement. Therefore it had been and in the 1960s was now again host to the Frankfurt Institute for Social Research, famous for its neo-Marxist, psychoanalytically informed social theory. Having given up on what my only supportive professor at the time called "the antifeminist profession" of history, I had escaped to Frankfurt to study philosophy and social theory with the remaining professors of the Frankfurt institute. Once there, I had become deeply involved in the student movement's project to create new forms of early childhood education, an effort which sought a viable alternative to the authoritarian traditions of German fascism by renewing the psychoanalytic pedagogy of the 1920s (best known here in the work of Bernfeld and Reich) establishing "antiauthoritarian" early childhood centers. Yet at the same time, my commitment to the new wave of feminism was leading to an inexorable break with my first psychoanalyst, a man whose antifascist history still did not prepare him for the idea of angry women writing attacks on the idea of penis envy and the myth of the vaginal orgasm.

---

[1] The story of Bertha Papenheim's treatment with Breuer is a complicated one. As Appignanesi and Forrester (1992) detail, Freud's later account of it suggests that Breuer terminated the treatment when his patient, purportedly at the end of abreacting all her symptoms, called for him to return and announced that Dr. B.'s baby was coming. In any event, contrary to the account in the *Studies*, Pappenheim was in and out of sanitorium for a number of years with continued symptoms. Freud's correspondence with Martha at that time seems to indicate that they were already aware of the possibility of attraction on the part of physician or patient, and also of Frau Breuer's jealousy.

The Primal Leap of Psychoanalysis, From Body to Speech

The inception of the women's movement brought the dialectical poles of psychoanalysis and feminism into violent contradiction, seemingly the contradiction between the acknowledgement of social oppression and the awareness of internal repression. The notion of rebellion opposed the notion of illness, making heroines, or at least protesters, out of patients. Not surprisingly, hysteria was among the first issues explored by feminist criticism, and the idea of the hysteric as an antecedent form of woman's protest against the constraints of the patriarchal family (Cixous & Clement, 1975; see also Bernheimer & Kahane, 1985; Showalter, 1985;) was among the earliest revisions proposed by feminist scholarship.

Significant for our inquiry, however, is the fact that her illness is not the only thing for which Bertha Pappenheim is remembered in Frankfurt today. Pappenheim, founder of the first feminist Jewish women's organization, is not as well-known as her alter ego Anna O. But her history, with pictures, is to be found in the *Woman's Guide to Frankfurt* (Hillman, 1992), packed in alongside reminiscences of our contemporary women's movement as well as articles on women in health, banking and the performing arts. Pappenheim's address to the German women's congress in Berlin, 1912, can be found in the volumes on the history of Jewish women in Germany recently published by the state of Hessen (Wagner, Mehrwald, Maierhof, Jansen 1994). Here Pappenheim analyzes the difficult position of Jewish women, deprived of access to their own religious tradition, denied instruction in the Hebrew language and texts, prevented from managing even those institutions most relevant to them.

In recalling Pappenheim's history it is not my intention to create a countermyth of the feminist heroine or to take an uncritical feminist revisionist version of hysteria at face value. For reading Pappenheim's words is not an unmixed experience. Both as she appears to us in Breuer's recorded recollection and in the later histories that see her as the founder of the German Jewish women's movement and a forerunner of modern social work, Pappenheim is surely a difficult figure with whom to identify. A woman who saw the straight lines of needlepoint as a metaphor for the well-lived, socially useful life (Hillman, 1992), who renounced sexual freedom in favor of social agency, she was a woman guided by an incredibly powerful super ego. Nonetheless it was she who became a rebel against the role of women prescribed by her religion and family, who did not finally remain paralyzed by unexpressed anger and desire, who strove valiantly to express them through her body and her speech. One could say that she overcame her incapacity by developing a position of active mastery in the world—a reversal which, in Freud's thought, would count as the characteristic masculine strategy for overcoming hysteria (Freud, 1896).

The reversal of passivity and the overcoming of the feminine position will turn out to be quite important, indeed fateful, to psychoanalysis. Pappenheim herself promulgated a feminism that founded women's active position in the virtues of maternal care as well as in economic independence and self-expression, the right to which she defended eloquently along with the right to freedom from sexual exploitation. Appignanesi and Forrester (1992) call the transformation from the illness of Anna O. to the healthy activity of Pappenheim "an inexplicable discontinuity." In fact, one could easily see her effort to forget her past, to repudiate her identity as patient and assume that of an activist social worker as a kind of defensive reaction. Then again, one could say that it reflects an identification with the other side of the analytic couple, the position of healer and helper, an identification Freud himself would later propose as a means of cure.

As historical figures, Pappenheim and Freud inhabit the same discursive world, the tradition of German Enlightenment and humanism that secularized Judaism had made its own. In one respect their assessment of women's condition matched: Even as Pappenheim saw the one possibility for equal self-expression and agency in the maternal, Freud too defined the maternal position as the one in which women are active rather than passive. However, the gap between their positions becomes evident when we consider Pappenheim's declaration (1912) that the only commandment that gives women a position equal to that of men in the Jewish community is the one that constitutes the main tenet of the Jewish religion, "Love thy Neighbor as thyself," the very commandment that Freud (1930) uses to illustrate the naivete of religion and the nature of reaction formation. The disjunction between Pappenheim and Freud marks the site of a tension between psychoanalysis and feminism regarding love and femininity: For Freud, love is to be deconstructed, revealing the terms of sexuality or libido—yet this endeavor will be fraught with the contradiction between the effort to identify woman's hidden desire and his relegation of her desire to passivity; for Pappenheim, altruistic love is to be liberated from a desire associated with sexual passivity and exploitation into a protective identification (or identifying protection) with the vulnerable Other. If you like, the tension between these positions may be seen as constituting an unfortunate kind of choice, one that has pulled feminist writers on hysteria in opposing directions (Bernheimer & Kahane, 1985; Gallop, 1982; Rose, 1985): On the one hand, reliance on Freud's attempt to liberate us from ideal forms of love; on the other, an effort to reinhabit and so revalue the position of the cast-off other.

Observing these pulls and counterpulls in the history of feminist thought, one might well ask, What does it mean, in light of Pappenheim's trajectory, to found feminism in a flight from the primary leap into the arms of the male healer, from the unanalyzed, un-worked-through erotic transference? But my focus will be on psychoanalysis, its founding in a particular constellation in which femininity becomes imbricated with passivity. Does not this, too, reflect a flight from the erotic, from the confrontation with female sexuality? This essay, therefore, will query psychoanalysis, concentrating on the ambivalent legacy Freud bequeathed us, a kind of liberation, freedom from religious and moral strictures, from grand ideals, from the temptation to save and redeem—but offered at a price: denial of the analyst's subjectivity and desire which might mirror that of the patient; distance from the helpless, the passive, and for that matter, the feminine Other, identification with whom did not always come easily to Freud, did not fit with his notion of objectivity and science. (Although it will follow from his own thinking that such identification is ineluctable and can only be prevented by acting against it in some intrapsychic way.) Thus I shall ask, How has the history of psychoanalysis been marked by the move from passivity to activity, and how is this move fundamental to the problems of the transference, especially the transference between unequal persons—doctor and patient, male authority and woman rebel? How did Freud's way of formulating that move reflect his ambivalence about attributing activity to women (see Hoffman, 1996), especially sexual activity, and incorporate defensive aspects that the psychoanalytic project must continually bring to consciousness?

Beginning with the *Studies*, the issues of passive versus active—along with other complementarities such as identification or distance, empathy or objectivity—can be seen as gender underliners of the themes that recurrently trouble the evolution of psychoanalysis. The effort to clarify those themes, to overcome an old and shallow opposition between feminism and psychoanalysis, might be seen as the work of producing a more creative tension

5

between the seemingly disparate personas, Anna and Bertha. So if psychoanalysis asks of femininism that it interrogate a founding gesture of liberation that denies the truth of dependency and desire, feminism asks of psychoanalysis that it reconsider its historical positioning of its Other, the one who is not yet able to speak for herself. Let us remind ourselves that in front of Salpetriere, where Charcot paraded his hysterics as a spectacle for popular audiences, stands a statue of Pinel freeing the mad from their chains; indeed, Freud noted at the time that this scene was painted on the wall of that very lecture theater (Showalter, 1985). Doesn't that irony enjoin such a reconsideration?

In our time, this reconsideration has led to a concern with the radical effects of perspective, the necessity of struggling to grasp the viewpoint of another as well as to strain our own view through the critical filter of analysis. Easily said, but not easily done. Seeking to grasp the real process involved in attaining an approximation of another's viewpoint (or even glimpses of it) as well as awareness of our own subjective view is central to our current efforts to elaborate an intersubjective psychoanalysis. Hopefully, we shall reach some clarification of what this means by the end of this essay. Provisionally, I will say that grasping the other's viewpoint means striving to dissolve the complementary opposition of the subject and object that inevitably appeared and reappears in the practice and theory of psychoanalysis. As I shall try to show, Freud's work, beginning with the *Studies*, aspired to move beyond the evident constraints of this complementarity, but was nevertheless continually drawn back into that opposition because of the confluence of scientific rationalism and gender hierarchy.

If we, in hindsight, are more aware of what pulls us back into that complementarity, we are also more inclined to identify with Bertha's position in the story. This is not only because our theory of the unconscious teaches us that we cannot prevent such identification, that we can only split it off, repudiate it, in effect dislocate it and thus create a dangerous form of complementarity (one which, indeed, allows only a choice between immediate, unthinking, "hysterical" identification or repudiation). It is also the contribution of both contemporary feminism and psychoanalysis to our understanding of the necessity of taking in the position of the other. As a result, we recognize that the only choice is to develop this identification, that the (re)admission of what was rejected is central to evolving the analyst's position as well as the patient's. The dialectic by which we undo repudiation is as important to psychoanalysis as it has been to the project of women's liberation, as it has been to each of the successive demands for recognition articulated in this century by the silenced or excluded.

The process by which demands are raised against those who already claim to be empowered as rational, speaking subjects is not identical with psychoanalysis. Nonetheless, the movement of psychoanalysis has a certain parallel with this project, which requires the self-conscious consideration of how to develop its forms of identification. As we see in social movements that found new identities, demands for recognition have their problematic side—a kind of entitlement or moral absolutism, which is always inextricable from and fueled by the power it opposes (see Chapter 3). It therefore always draws the other into the relationship of reversible complementarity. In many ways, as I shall try to show, Freud's journey through the transference is an allegory of learning to traverse the unmapped and surprising (though oddly familiar) paths of such complementary relationships.

II

Lest the comparisons I have drawn between the movement of psychoanalysis and that of feminism seem forced, let me delay consideration of the history of the transference a moment and consider the background of psychoanalysis in relation to European thought. Our consciousness of who we are today should take into account the history of psychoanalysis as a practice indebted to the project of liberation rooted in the Enlightenment—and Freud, despite all his political skepticism, surely did see psychoanalysis as an activity only thinkable through and because of the Enlightenment project of personal freedom, rational autonomy, being for oneself. This project, as Kant described in "What is Enlightenment," is that of freedom from tutelage, in German *Unmundigkeit*. Usually translated as "attaining majority, adulthood," the term *Mundig*, derived from the word for mouth, refers to speaking for oneself (in fact, Pappenheim [12] uses it when she points out that every thirteen-year-old Jewish boy receives a *Mundigsprechung*, which girls are denied). To be *mundig* is to be entitled, empowered to speak, the opposite term to the one so often used today: silenced. It may thus fairly be understood as the antithesis of hysterical passivity, speechlessness. For the better part of the twentieth century this project of freedom from authority has been questioned precisely because—so the poststructural, postmodern critique goes—the subject of speech was never intended to be all-inclusive, was always predicated on the exclusion of an other, an abject, a disenfranchised, or an object of speech. And yet, precisely this critique of exclusion and objectification operates by referring back to a demand for inclusive recognition of subjectivity that the Enlightenment project formulated (Benjamin, 1994, Chapter 3).

Now this contradiction, between rejecting and calling upon the categories of Enlightenment, makes for a particular uneasiness regarding the place of psychoanalysis. For the twentieth-century theory that rejects the Enlightenment has invoked Freud himself in its efforts to show that the figure of the autonomous, coherent, rational subject is a deceptive appearance, which serves to deny the reality of a fragmented, chaotic, incoherent self, whose active efforts to articulate and make meaning are ultimately defensive. And yet the advocacy of meaning over chaos, thought over suffering, integration over splitting, symbolization over symptom, consciousness over unconsciousness remains essential to psychoanalysis. Finally, we can cite one more problem, one which arises regarding the psychoanalytic relationship: The achievement of autonomy is revealed to be the product of a discourse that situates the subject in the oppositional complementarities—subject and object, mind and body, active and passive, autonomously rational and "irrational"—that worked historically by splitting off the devalued side of the opposition from the subject. And, of course, by associating femininity with the devalued side. Psychoanalysis has thus continually reenacted these oppositions, which are in fact iterations of gender hierarchy, even as it offers the possibility of uncovering their meanings. As with Freud's frequent rehearsals and disclaimers of the association between passivity and femininity, psychoanalysis reproduces the splits it aims to analyze.

Thus, to pick up where I left off, it is useful to explore the identification with Anna O./Bertha Pappenheim because she incarnates for the first time and in a most compelling way that dual identity which each psychoanalyst-patient pair, separately and together, must embody. The contradictions of Anna/Bertha—which appear through the split image of the helpless, fragmented patient versus the articulate, stalwart feminist who defends the helpless—reflect the split in every analyst, who is her/himself subject to as well as subject of the analytic process. In Freud's own evolution as well as in psychoanalysis in general, we can see the problem of constructing the encounter as one between the Analyst-Subject who already speaks and the Patient-Other who does not yet speak for herself. This suffering Other requires recognition by the subject who does speak. But this recognition will be effective only if it incorporates a moment of identification, and so disrupts the enclosed identity of the Subject. Likewise, the Other's attainment of speech may only proceed by her identification with the speaking subject, by which she is in danger of losing her own "identity" as Other. If the patient must "become" the analyst, the analyst must also "become" the patient.

Thus both analyst and patient have reason to resist the identifications that result from their encounter, for eventually the doubleness of identification leads to a breakdown of the rationalistic complementarities between knower and known, active and helpless, subject and object. And while this identification may in theory be laudably subversive of hierarchy, it is in practice a "most dangerous method" (Kerr, 1993), generating a muddle of boundaries, mystification, anxiety and old defenses against it. To this analytic heart of darkness we will turn shortly. For now, speaking of theory, let us say that psychoanalysis and feminism may join in the project of inspiring this inevitable breakdown to assume a creative rather than destructive form—to challenge the valorization of the autonomous, active, "masculine" side of the gender polarity without reactively elevating its opposite.

I am highlighting this paradoxical movement in psychoanalytic history: That even in the moment of breaking down those oppositions through which the masculine subject was constituted, the psychoanalytic project necessarily participated in the hierarchical opposition between activity and passivity with its gender implications. This project, raising the symptom to articulation in the symbol, I have designated here as the primary move from the body into speech, referring to this founding form of psychoanalytic activity as the "primal leap," punning on the German word for origin, *Ur-Sprung*, *Sprung* meaning leap and *Ur* meaning original, primal, first, deepest. From body to speech. To make the inarticulate articulate, to translate the symptomatic gestures of the body into language, is incontrovertibly the first lesson of Freud and Breuer's work.

No sooner having said this, however, we must object, or at least ask, Whose speech? For the leap that is psychoanalysis consists, properly speaking, in Freud's decision to give up hypnosis in favor of a more collaborative enterprise, one in which the patient herself

9

becomes the *subject* of speech—-and if Freud chose to attribute this transition to a certain resistance on the part of his patients (Breuer & Freud, 1895), perhaps in order to legitimate it as a necessity (or to occlude his fear of the erotic transference that hypnosis unleashed, as his autobiography revealed [Appignanesi & Forrester, 1992], this makes the sharing of credit no less true.

How else could the value of collaboration be discovered, if not through the patient's refusal of the passive position of being hypnotized, even if that refusal appeared to be a resistance? In effect, the step out of passivity is framed as resistance. Subjected to her own symptoms and captive in her own body, the patient can nonetheless mobilize against surrender of consciousness. And so the origin of psychoanalysis, its decisive move, is ambiguous.

I hope here merely to underscore a certain paradox in the evolution of psychoanalysis as a discipline, and in each individual analysis as well—each fresh resistance of the patient drives the process forward. To refer to the thermodynamic metaphors of the nineteenth century, we could say that the resistance is the essential element in the combustion that drives the engine of change. For Freud himself, this paradox was exemplified in his discovery that the repressing agent was itself repressed, that the "secrets" of the psychic world seemed increasingly to lie not in the content of the repressed, in other words, not merely in what the resistance hides, but in the resistance itself. Resistance itself becomes the revelation, as in Freud's discovery of the function of erotic transference, or any acting in the transference—but more of that later.

So far I have been constructing a leading argument here, suggesting that the move from the body that suffers itself to be an instrument of unconscious communication to the speaking subject who articulates insight seems to fit with a transition to active subjectivity as long-defined by the Enlightenment tradition. Thus Freud framed his understanding of overcoming resistance and defence in the *Studies* in characteristic fashion:

> What means have we at our disposal for overcoming this continual resistance? Few, but they include almost all those by which one man can exert a psychical influence on another . . . we may reckon on the intellectual interest which the patient begins to feel after working for a short time. By explaining things to him, by giving him information about the marvelous world of psychical processes into which we ourselves only gained in-

10

sight by such analyses, we make him himself a collaborator, in-
duce him to regard himself with the objective interest of an investigator, and thus push back his resistance. . . . One works to
the best of one's power as an elucidator, teacher, representative
of a freer or superior view of the world, as a father confessor
giving sympathy and absolution. . . . for it is well to recognize
this clearly: the patient gets free from the hysterical symptom
by reproducing the pathogenic impressions that caused it and
by giving utterance to them with an expression of affect, and
thus the therapeutic task consists solely in inducing him to do
so. When once this task has been accomplished there is nothing
left for the physician to correct or remove. (282–283)

So we see, the analyst has merely set the patient free, has in
fact found a way to make him (Nota bene! when the patient is active, Freud uses the male pronoun; when simply ill, he uses the feminine) a collaborator. The patient is to identify with the analyst in the
overcoming of resistance through self-reflection, a process of internalization that implies both tutelage and freedom from tutelage. He
is to collaborate in an investigation. By contrast, Breuer's use of hypnosis with Anna O. seems of a piece with his medicating her, case
managing her in the manner appropriate to the metaphor of an illness, still embedded in a discourse of subject and object, actor and
acted-upon. Such a discourse, sustained by the practice of hypnosis,
could only explore the patient's subjectivity by vitiating it of the
qualities that otherwise characterize it: agency and intentionality.

Of course, the transition from passivity to activity, from symptoms to being the subject of speech, turned out to be not a one-time
leap, but a process that Freud evolved slowly, for which the giving
up of hypnosis was only a beginning. Indeed, we can see Freud's
subsequent elaboration of psychoanalytic practice as an ongoing effort to remove the analyst from the position of coercive authority
and to enfranchise the patient.

But even as Freud reports his move away from hypnosis, he allows us to discern the way that the patient exerted her power to
bring into being another force. This, the force of transference, is already discernible, already beginning to destabilize the main event of
the *Studies*. This event was meant to be Freud's discovery of a for-
mulaic equation: one symptom, one recollection. In any event, it is
apparent in the first study that symptoms are not the only matter at
hand. For it is not merely in her body that Anna O. offers up the en-

coded memories; equally important are the reliving of perceptions and feelings. These Freud will later figure as the main thing opposing language: "acting," a term that evokes not merely doing, but dramatizing, representing in deed. When Anna O. refuses to drink water because it reminds her of the despised dog who drank from the bowl, this is not a bodily symptom, but acting.

Where speech, symbolic articulation, would constitute the true activity of the subject, acting has been seen as merely another form of representing without knowing what is being represented, of evacuating or expelling, hence not an expression of subjectivity. This distinction between communicating and acting is still subscribed to by many analysts, for instance Green (1986). Yet, acting has also been seen as a stage between discharge and full representation (Freedman, 1985) that implicates the analyst in a new way. In fact, in contemporary relational analysis, acting and interacting are the indispensable medium through which the analytic work proceeds. At the very least, acting constitutes a new intermediate position between unconscious and conscious, a different kind of effort at representation, which at once reveals and resists—to paraphrase what Winnicott says about destruction, it is only resistance because of our liability not to understand it, to become caught up in it.

Freud was at first sanguine about seizing this new opportunity for mastery through understanding. For although the patient, Freud tells us, is "deceived afresh every time this is repeated . . . the whole process followed a law" (Breuer & Freud, 1895, 303–304). The work follows a "law," the law of logic, the same law formulated for relieving symptoms through images or pictures produced under pressure: As soon as the images have been put into words, fully explicated, raised to the symbolic level, they disappear. In the same way, Freud contends, the illusion of the transference "melts away" once he makes the nature of the obstacle clear. Freud has not yet confronted the intersubjective aspect of the phenomenon, the bidirectionality of unconscious communication; he believes that transference can be simply observed from without. He remains reassuringly within the law—according to which words must replace action, symbol replace symptom, each proceeding in order.

Freud's remarks at the end of the *Studies* on resistance and transference in the absence of hypnosis already represent an important modification of his enthusiastic statements in the Preliminary Communication of 1893. Still, they continue to echo the earlier optimistic formula in which symptom dispersal occurs by putting the event and affect into words. Once the activity of speech—language—substitutes for action of the body or of the transference, everything follows. Where before the patient's resistance was overcome by the pressure of the physician's hand, now the patient must be more consciously enlisted to overcome her own resistance.

Freud's move away from hypnosis is of a piece with a gradual process of lessening the doctor's grip on the patient's mental activity, of relinquishing coercion and control by the doctor, with a concomitant freeing of the analysand, whose autonomy should be realized within the analysis itself. Already, we have glimpsed the contradictions within the discourse of autonomy, and it should not surprise us that Freud continues to struggle with them, that the new technique does not remove these contradictions but *displaces them in the transference*. In his writings on the transference more than a decade later, we will observe in new form the reinstituting of the hierarchical binaries that have been so readily exposed in the paradigm of male doctor, female hysteric. Indeed, the transference gathers these contradictions together in a way that led Freud to the apt metaphor of explosive chemicals.

In "Remembering, Repeating and Working Through" (1914), Freud looks backward on the path he has followed in order to relinquish charismatic authority, hypnotism and faith-healing: the beginning use of interpretation to "circumvent resistance" while still focusing on the symptom, followed by replacing abreaction with "the expenditure of work which the patient had to make" to suspend his criticism of free association "in accordance with the fundamental rule . . . and finally . . . the consistent technique used today, in which the analyst gives up the attempt to bring a particular moment or problem into focus . . . studying whatever is present for the time being on the surface of the patient's mind" and using interpretation mainly to recognize resistances and make them known to the patient. "From this there results a new sort of division of labor," in which the doctor uncovers resistance and the patient fills in the material. But, Freud avers, "the aim of these different techniques has, of course, remained the same . . . . to fill in gaps in memory; dynamically speaking, it is to overcome resistances due to repression" (147).

Freud's narrative constructs a consistent, logically proceeding evolution of his method and aims. Notwithstanding this coherence, there are some significant points of difference between these later writings on transference and his earlier formulations in *The Interpretation of Dreams*. In particular, this is evident in his ideas regarding the surrender of the critical function of reason. In *The Interpretation of Dreams* Freud tells us that

> We must aim at bringing about two changes in the patient: an increase in the attention he pays to his own psychical percep- tions and the elimination of the criticism by which he normally sifts the thoughts that occur to him. . . . It is necessary to insist explicitly on his renouncing all criticism of the thoughts that he perceives. We therefore tell him that the success of the psycho- analysis depends on his noticing and reporting whatever comes into his head. . . . He must adopt a completely impartial attitude to what occurs to him. (101)

Freud emphasizes the importance of *"relaxing deliberate (and no doubt critical) activity,"* of allowing ideas to emerge "of their own free will" (102). And here, following a suggestion made by Rank, who was particularly identified with the tradition of romanticism and its aes- thetic reflections, he invokes Schiller, who explained to a friend that his inability to be creative probably lay

> in the constraint imposed by your reason upon your imagina- tion. . . . [I]t seems a bad thing and detrimental to the creative work of the mind if Reason makes too close an examination of the ideas as they come pouring in—at the very gateway, as it were. . . . where there is a creative mind, Reason . . . relaxes its watch upon the gates, and the ideas rush in pell-mell, and only then does it look them through and examine them in a mass. You critics . . . are ashamed or frightened of the momentary and transient extravagances which are to be found in all truly cre- ative minds. . . . You complain of your unfruitfulness because you reject too soon and discriminate too severely. (103)

"What Schiller describes as a relaxation of the watch upon the gates of Reason," Freud says, is not all that difficult. He then goes on to discuss the two psychical agencies or forces, first the wish, ex- pressed in the dream, which corresponds to the Imagination; then the censor, the gate, which corresponds to Reason.

This text expresses what might be considered the first of Freud's two, antithetical theories of mental freedom: The first pro- posal advocates a freedom from the critical faculty responsible for resistance, allowing the real, in other words, unconscious, thoughts to emerge. The second theory, that emerges in his later writings on transference, emphasizes the freedom that comes in reorienting the mind to the reality principle and relieving it of preoccupations with unconscious thoughts that hold it captive to the past and the pleasure principle. It may even be said that Reason, for Freud, has a very different status when it opposes the aesthetic imagination than when it opposes instinct, when the conflict relates to self-expression (his own, especially) or when it relates to the transference.

Now in the beginning, Freud intended that the patient abandon his critical faculty and, in effect, turn it over to the analyst, who retains a logical, organizing mentation, noting the logic of dream thoughts, following gaps and clues. In a sense, the division of labor here involves the alignment of the patient with the first psychic agency, imagination, and the doctor with the second, discriminating Reason. But soon Freud came to recognize that deliberate attention is as problematic for the analyst as for the patient. It is after he has formulated his theory of dream interpretation that he comes to realize that inner, mental freedom is necessary for the analyst, to prevent him from controlling the patient, and so losing the access to repressed material that would be gained from the patient's obeying the fundamental rule. We may speculate that Freud attained this realization through hard experience, his failure in Dora's case.

The case of Dora, we know, was the one Freud hoped would actualize his dream theory, but which, instead, came to exemplify the transferential difficulties that ensue when the analyst tries to retain all logic and reason on his side. It is easy to read Dora as an object lesson in the catastrophic results of attacking the resistance in the way Freud originally and naively recommended, of controlling the locus of attention in order to create a seamless narrative of cause and effect. Freud was disappointed in his expectation that Dora would, as he wrote to Fliess, "smoothly open to the existing collection of picklocks" (1900, 427).

Dora has been understood by a multitude of authors to encapsulate what is problematic in any simplified understanding of bringing the hysterical patient to speech. Unlike Anna O., Dora and the unnamed female homosexual both reveal, more than Freud seemed to intend, a conflict in which Freud tries to penetrate woman's sexuality but the woman resists or rebels. If Freud (1905) thinks that he who disdains the key, which is sexuality, will never open the door to the patient's mind, then Dora, as Jane Gallop (1985) remarks, is there to let him know that no one wants to be opened by a skeleton key.

15

Feminists and psychoanalysts alike have pointed out the way in which Freud pursued the unlocking of meaning, the mining of secrets, the connecting of event and symptom in a seamless narrative—without gaps and holes, or other feminine metaphors of incomplete knowledge (Moi, 1985)—to the detriment of the analytic stance toward the patient.

In any event, the recognition of the transference, Dora's particularly "pointed" resistance, once again pushed Freud to reflect on his position and abandon a certain form of control. He moved toward the model of evenly suspended attention as he described in his own retrospective account. Nonetheless—and here we come to Freud's "second theory"—Freud seems to reproduce the conflict between reason and imagination on a new level in his writings on the transference between 1912 and 1915. The old refrain of the conflict between language and action can be heard in his discussion of struggle between "intellect and instinct, recognition and the striving for discharge"(1912, 108). Yet again the problem emerges that action is indispensable, for "No one can be slain in absentia, in effigy" (108). Thus in order to put an end to the unconscious manipulation of the powerful forces, we must expand our permission, invite the patient to take certain liberties—not just the relaxation of judgment and freedom of thoughts, but now the actual reenactment in the transference in "the intermediate realm" or "playground" of the analytic situation (Freud, 1914).

At the same time, the analyst must be able to go near the dark forces without succumbing to them, protect himself from the patient's effort to assert "her irresistibility, to destroy the physician's authority by *bringing him down to the level of the lover* [my italics]" (1915b, 163). And "to overcome the pleasure principle . . . to achieve this *mastery* of herself she must . . . [be led to] that greater *freedom* within the mind which distinguishes conscious mental activity [my italics]" (170). As I've said elsewhere (Benjamin, 1995b), paradoxically the patient's autonomy emerges out of the identification with the analyst's authority, which she accepts. *She* makes the axiomatic move from loving him as an object to identification and puts him in place of her ego ideal.

But this is a dangerous project, and Freud (1915b) must justify his persistence in unleashing the explosive forces. As he does so often, he looks for legitimation not in the freedom of imagination, but in science, the discourse of objectivity, of reason over instinct. He compares the handling of the transference to the chemist who carefully handles the dangerous chemicals in the laboratory. Of course, the problem

16

with this analogy is that the chemist is not the chemical, whereas the analyst does act as a force in the combustion of the transference. The psychoanalytic doctor is less like a chemist than like the priest who must encounter the demonic in order to exorcise it. Indeed, it turns out that psychoanalysis can refuse hypnotism and faith-healing precisely because the same force reappears in the transference—as Freud (1921) will say later, it is only a step from being in love to hypnotism. For that matter, how could any German-speaker miss the connections between healing, (*heilen*) holy (*heilig*) and redeemer (*heiland*)?

III

What Freud's warnings scarcely conceal is the impossibility of the very objectivity that he prescribes. As these connections suggest, the psychoanalytic doctor is not able to heal without becoming implicated in the transference, and so in the illness itself. This could be the message to analysts offered by Kafka's story, "A Country Doctor": a story written as though in response to Freud, or perhaps, a doctor's dream. The doctor is called out to a distant village at night, but he has no horses of his own to pull his wagon. Seemingly in exchange for the team of horses that mysteriously appears in his barnyard, he must leave at home his maid, Rosa, to be raped by the groom who appeared along with the horses. While he is objecting, the horses simply carry him off. In a moment he arrives at the village, is surrounded by the patient's family and neighbors, who press him toward the patient, a young boy lying in bed who hardly appears ill, perhaps a malingerer. But as the doctor would leave he looks closer and discovers the patient is truly ill, he has a gaping wound in his side, pink—that is to say Rosa—which is alive with little worms (maggots). The family grab him, undress him and lay him in bed, while outside the school choir sings, "Unclothe him, Unclothe him, then he will heal, and should he not heal, then kill him. He's only a doctor, only a doctor." But he, "thoroughly collected and above it all," simply looks at them. As he escapes naked, his coat hanging from his carriage, the villagers triumph, "Rejoice you patients, the doctor has been put in bed with you." Still, as he flees, he knows his practice will go to pieces, he will never recover, his Rosa is sacrificed, and the stable groom is still rampaging in his house.

We might consider this dream-story to evoke something of the danger Freud would have had in mind when he admonished young physicians to heal by remaining covered, true to their cloth. To become unclothed, naked, is be de-vested of one's authority, brought down to the patient's level. It is thus to have the parts of the self that have been split off into the patient—one's own dangerous instincts—exposed. Unavoidably, to face the way in which one's authority has been created out of this very process of projection. To be clothed, in-vested, is to have this process remain invisible, and in a sense to protect the authority of the official, the clergyman, the father, the physician, from exposure (Santner, 1996).

If the patient and the doctor speak a dialogue that is actually made of two voices within one mind, still they are in competition with each other for space (You're crowding my deathbed, says the boy) as well as recognition or pity (What should I do? believe me, it's not easy for me either, replies the doctor. I'm supposed to be satisfied with that excuse/apology? complains the boy.) The doctor consoles him by suggesting that his wound is something others never get to have: "many offer their side, and never even hear the axe in the forest, let alone have it approach them." Then the doctor snaps out of it. Too late, his authority can never be recovered.

As the symmetry of their dialogue implies, the level of action here reflects a complementarity that, like the erotic transference, first requires and then risks the analyst's authority. We might better grasp this form of complementarity by referring to a distinction well-known in the detective genre (Zizek, 1991). In the *Studies*, Freud is still in the mode of Holmes, the investigator who is "collected and above it all," who has a collection of picklocks and an eagle eye for holes in others' stories, who intends to construct a seamless narrative to which he knows the culprit will surrender. She will be able to object no further, she will have to admit the truth of her desire. Then there is the Noir detective, Marlowe or Spade for instance, who gets involved and is implicated in the whole story, and if he in the end places the guilt where it belongs and refuses to take the fall with the guilty one, still, like the country doctor, he is not untouched—indeed, he is never quite the same. This might be seen as the passage Freud has to suffer in the Dora case, from a complementarity that establishes well-bounded opposites, to the reversible complementarity of "It takes one to know one," the one that takes you into bed with the patient.

Freud's difficulty in accepting his identification with the passive, helpless position of the young woman Dora, struggling against her reduction to the position of object, leads him into the reversible complementarity of the power struggle. (More profoundly, Rose [1985] argues, recognizing Dora's rejection of him in favor of Frau K.'s adorable white body would destabilize Freud's theory of sexuality and femininity; it would reveal a more complex constellation in which Dora, or anyone, could both identify with and love the same object. This would disrupt the very framework of heterosexual gender complentarity, and in effect *drag* him into the feminine identification he resists.) He becomes the complementary other to Dora's resistance not only by identifying with Herr K. but by becoming invested in proving that he knows what is really going on. One of the most striking points in his narration is the way that his own observation in the text—that one always reproaches the other with that which one does oneself—applies to his own ending: He reproaches Dora with wishing only to take revenge, while one can hardly see his refusal to treat her on that ground as any less vengeful. Dora's resistance, her cool rejection of Freud's perfect interpretations that mimics the rhetorical position of the scientific authority with its object helpless before it—like his unnamed "female homosexual" (Harris, 1991)—undermines his vestments of neutrality by provoking him to reveal his investment.

The patient who acts, rather than thinks or speaks, pulls the analyst into the complementary identification and away from both representation and empathy. The analyst who resists identification with the patient's position engages the complementary aspect of the relationship and unwittingly stimulates action. The patient's action then becomes, painfully, an inverted mirror of the analyst's action that aspires to achieve through knowing or helping a security-in-control. As Racker (1968) made clear, the complementary position can be countered by the identificatory position in the countertransference, the analyst's ability to be on both sides of the divide. By adopting the concordant position of identification with the patient's position, the analyst has the leverage to think about the patient. If the analyst does not identify with the patient in her or his own ego, "recognizing what belongs to the other as one's own," (134) she or he will become identified with the patient's bad or good objects, and the split complementarity ensues: doer/done to, vengeful/victimized, etc.

What does it mean to identify in one's own ego? In a sense, it means the opposite of hysterical identification, which involves a "mapping" (J. Mitchell, 1995) of self onto the other, an unmediated assimilation of other and self that Freud writes of in the *Interpretation* and later classifies as a phenomenon like mass contagion (1921).

Such hysterical identification—which may be part of the inevitable feeling evoked by the relationship with certain patients and which we can sometimes only divest by cloaking ourselves with our role— can be distinguished from those identifications that are mediated by representation and so eventually become useful sources of knowledge for us and the patient. Another way to formulate this is to say that, properly speaking, not the act of identification, which is unavoidable and unthought, but the act of representing identification creates a point of freedom.[2]

In practice, we also distinguish identification that retains contact with the patient's multiple and conflicting positions from the kind that appears in split complementarities, in which we take one side of a conflict. As we see in Dora, the notion that enemies resemble each other applies, perhaps because the patient is also identified with the bad objects in her ego. Following the unconscious logic of "I could be you and you could be me," complementarity often involves symmetrical responses, tit for tat, I'm rubber you're glue. Thus the complementary countertransference recreates an internal dialogue, as in Kafka's dream-story, which captures both participants. Insofar as the patient experiences the analyst's investment in being the one who "understands rather than the one who is understood, who is needed rather than who needs" (Hoffman, 1991), to be the master or Lacan's "subject supposed to know," the analyst may find her or himself pulled ever deeper into the power struggle. In such a case, when the analyst is in-vested in omniscience, the basic fault in the idea of the patient making the analyst into her/his ego ideal is exposed.

---

[2] This distinction leads to an important point regarding unconscious representation and its relation to trauma, in particular in relation to actual events. Since traumatic events are dissociated, that is, remain split off, encapsulated, they often remain concrete and unsymbolized, not susceptible to being grasped metaphorically. Identifications developed around such experiences are thus nonsymbolic, immediate, and also subject to the logic of primitive reversibility, "If I am this, you are this; if you are that, I am that." This is a principle that Casement (1991) has discussed in reference to Mate-Blanco's idea of symmetry as part of the logic of the unconscious, and indeed the unconscious is often reduced to this logic. But it may be more helpful to think of this logic as not necessarily pertaining to all unconscious thought, but thought especially related to unsymbolized or traumatic experience.

For this ego ideal of analytic understanding has, to varying degrees, already been constituted through split complementary structures that devalue the one who is speechless, passive, does not know, is needy, the object of pity, etc. What it means to pull ourselves out of such complementary power struggles by immersing ourselves in a very specific way, learning to swim in the countertransference rather than drown, can surely be seen as the psychoanalytic project of the last few decades of the century. Freud's notion that the patient could identify with the ideal side of analytic authority momentarily forgets the equally plausible reaction of rejecting authority: that the patient would also attack the analyst precisely because of her or his investment in the role of healer (against which Freud also warns) would call forth the hidden dimension of power in knowledge, which cannot win out against unreason without the usual consequences of subjugating a binary opposite.

IV

In drawing a line between hypnosis/suggestion and analysis aimed at freeing the patient's subjectivity Freud instituted a crucial paradigm for dealing with binaries. As we shall see regarding the idea of analyst as ego ideal, such simple opposites are likely to conceal or obscure the contradictions that inevitably arise in our practice. The strict equation of the analyst's distance and objectivity with the patient's freedom that Freud invoked seems to have been more successful in providing legitimation for psychoanalysis than it was in working with patients. A case in point is Riviere, whose reflections on the negative therapeutic reaction drew on her own experience with Jones and Freud and apparently inspired Freud's original discussion of that phenomenon (Kris, 1994). In a noteworthy essay, A. Kris (1994) has pointed out the dilemma that arises in Freud's (1923) efforts to address it, apparent in his footnote on the negative therapeutic reaction in *The Ego and the Id*. Freud remarks that successful work with a patient whose unconscious guilt leads to narcissistic defenses may "depend on whether the personality of the analyst allows of the patient's putting him in the place of his ego ideal, and this involves a temptation for the analyst to play the part of prophet, savior and redeemer to the patient" (1923, 50).

Kris believe this statement refers to Freud's decision to be more supportive in order to penetrate beneath the patient's critical attitude to the unconscious guilt, which Riviere herself saw as tied to depressive love for the lost, critical object. In other words, the supportive stance aims to steer clear of the inevitable complementarity that ensues when an attacking object is on the screen and either patient or analyst is impelled to play that object's part. To this aim the therapeutic move will be to achieve concordance, an identificatory position, what is commonly called empathy, and so steer clear of being attacker or attackee. But, Freud objects, this move will foster the patient's feeling that the analyst is now the savior from the critical object, will be loved in its place. What is to be done? In the very next sentence Freud objects to his own suggestion that the analyst's personality can play a role in counteracting the negative therapeutic reaction, stating that "the rules of analysis are diametrically opposed to the physician making use of his personality in any such manner." Characteristically, he refers us again to the aim of giving "the patient's ego *freedom* to choose. This, not making pathological reactions impossible, is the goal of analysis" (50, 1923, my italics).

It is noteworthy that Freud, in referring to what we now think of as the classical rules, does not distinguish between the analyst's countertransference fantasy of being a redeemer and the patient's fantasy of him as the savior in the transference. The countertransference reflects the analyst's disowned desire to be saved, projected onto the vulnerable, helpless patient. It is this unconscious identification with the wish to be saved that stimulates idealization, and sometimes enactment of the erotic transference very like the dynamic between Breuer and Anna. But the reaction against this desire, the superego's demand for abstinence, leads to other difficulties. For the idealization that devolves upon the analyst who abstains, who counters grandiosity and redemption with inpersonality, also produces a formidable ego ideal—and are we to think that just because the patient is to identify with that ideal the analyst does not appear as a different kind of "redeemer"? The history of sainthood in Christianity hardly supports such an assumption. This scenario produces the anti-erotic enactment in which the patient will have difficulties with the analyst's objective authority, will experience such adherence to rules as withholding, critical of her needs, and so reinstitute the analyst as a guilt-inducing object. We may question whether such withholding of subjective response makes the analyst less exalted (Menaker, 1942), less a god, especially to himself—and for the patient, certainly, he may well appear to be the god who denies only this particular sinner the redemption she seeks.

Freud sets up a parallel between two sets of contrasting terms: between remaining objective/abstinent and using one's own subjectivity, between falling into the temptation to be a redeemer/healer and giving the patient freedom. But these contrasts miss the crucial point of the analyst's identification with the patient and so lead Freud to an impasse—he should like to use his personality to prevent the punitive scenario but he would then lose his defense against the wish to play the redeemer—which he resolves not by analysis but by appealing to the rules. This paradigm of objectivity, with its conflation of subjectivity and idealization, failed to analyze the unconscious desire of the analyst. Holding sway for decades as a guide to those ensnared in the complementary transference, this view of the rules of analysis may well have created the problems it claimed to solve.

V

Doubtless the clinical impracticality of holding the position of objective knower as well as the influence of postmodern challenges to objectivist epistemologies have led to a profound revision in contemporary psychoanalytic thought, sometimes designated as intersubjective theory.[3] The idea of analytic neutrality is increasingly challenged (Renik, 1994) or subject to redefinition (Gerson, 1996a). The intersubjective analyst's idea of freedom—the analyst's freedom—is to make use of one's emotional responses, one's subjectivity, in a knowing way. Of course, contemporary analysts who identify with this position differ in the degree to which they support the patient, reveal their own process, and allow the idealizing transference to unfold. Analysts from a number of schools are beginning to argue that the analyst will not only experience in the countertransference all the possible positions that the coincidence of the patient's difficulties and analyst's disposition create, but will inevitably reveal some of this countertransference (Aron, 1996). In that case, the question will be whether this revelation is voluntary and controlled by the analyst, or happens "unconsciously," despite the analyst's efforts to avoid it.

---

[3] This is not the place to attempt a summary of such revisions, which include a range of relational, social-constructivist, perspectivist arguments by a wide range of analysts. A good summary can be found in Aron (1996).

To refigure what it means to use one's subjectivity rather than accept the polarity of subjectivity and objectivity is an important aim of contemporary analysis (Mitchell, 1993; Gill, 1994). We aim to formulate a space in between suggestion and objective distance, which encompasses the analyst's emotional response to the patient and takes account of her or his involvement in the complementarity transference action as well as the means for extricating her or himself from it. In the process, the distinction between speech and action necessarily breaks down (Greenberg, 1996; Aron, 1996), as we become aware that all speaking has the impact of an action and all action communicates "information" from a particular point of view. In other words, as we cease to privilege the analyst's perspective as objectively derived knowledge, we acknowledge the analyst's participation in an interaction of two subjects. The double action of intersubjectivity—recognizing the other's subjectivity and one's own—means that as the patient becomes less objectified, the analyst becomes a more "subjective" subject.

Such acknowledgement requires both a different understanding of mental structure, that is symbolic representation, and of the intersubjectivity of the analytic situation—each understanding furthering the other. The principle that informs both is the idea of transforming complementarities into dialectical tension, into tolerable paradox, instead of into antinomies that compel dangerous choices. Opposites are to some extent unavoidable because of the inherent psychic tendency to split; because, in fact, they allow the mind to think. It is the capacity to hold them in tension and overcome splitting that is at stake. This inevitable movement through opposites is what we need to hold in mind both in our theory and in the clinical situation.

Likewise, we may accept that the split complementarity inevitably reemerges time and again in the transference, and consider how we re-solve it in our minds, modify it by restoring the sense of separate subjectivities. Frequently this occurs not through distance, conventional objectivity, but by one person trying to know what the other is feeling, so that identification becomes a recognizable effort to break up the enclosure in the paranoid position. In this case, identification functions as a channel allowing the flow and processing of emotion (in self-psychological terms, through empathic introspection. Stolorow, Brandschaft & Atwood, 1987). To create the conditions for this flow, to establish this channel, the analyst must be able to think and represent the character of the current complementary situation, including her or his actions within it, as well as to simultaneously identify with unconscious communications from the patient as represented through her own responses (Spezzano, 1993).

If the complementary position is not supplemented by the represented identification, it will become sticky, intractable. The analyst will feel unable to think. The ability to symbolize emerges via the analyst's ability to survive the inevitable involvement in complementarity by making use of identificatory responses that bypass or dissolve it. The analyst is always striving to represent both the patient's position and her or his own in order to create the diclogic space of the third position. Even if this representation is at best only an approximation of the other's meaning, and at worst a misrepresentation, it can nevertheless serve to create the two planes necessary for the third, a double-sided perspective. It maintains a tension or space between self and other; it can be extended to the patient as an invitation to collaborative thinking. This intention can be felt by the parient and the content corrected. If I state flatly that misrecognition is a lesser danger, I believe it is the logical consequence of abandoning the ideal of objectivity in favor of acknowledging the analyst's subjectivity. Once subjectivity is embraced, we have entered into a realm of knowledge based on identifications, hence knowing that is intrapsychically filtered. In short, we must tolerate the inevitable misrecognition that accompanies our efforts at recognition. To react to this inevitability by relinquishing the effort to know or recognize would simply reinstall the principle of objective knowledge as the only one worth having.

VI

The psychoanalytic efforts to deconstruct the dominance of an objectively knowing subject in favor of a personal subjectivity parallel recent feminist efforts to disrupt the conventional oppositions and their encoding in gender hierarchies. The question of how we envision dissolving the ever-recurring complementarities, especially the idealizations intrinsic to binary hierarchies, is common to each. Some important overlaps can be found in the reassessment of the maternal function and of the maternal transferences that psychoanalysis and feminism have undertaken in the last decades. In rehabilitating maternal activity, both movements showed some propensity for idealization of the mother, an element I've pointed out in Pappenheim's feminism as well. While such idealization might have merely reproduced the logic of binary oppositions, reversing what was once devalued, they have actually allowed a far deeper exploration of maternal metaphors. With this, as we shall see, has come a perspective from which we can approach the questions of activity and passivity, body and speech, somewhat differently.

For example, we may now reverse the movement we followed in considering how psychoanalysis evolved its focus on symbolic function, which I have put in the shorthand "from body to speech." In a sense, much current work on early mother-infant interaction can be see as working backward from speech to the body, in its primary dimension as locus of sensation, energy and affect (see Brennan, 1992). In the thematic reworking of the body as container can be found a reprise, with a difference, of Freud's understanding of the body as energy system, of tension and discharge, of releasing affect through symptom-symbols. I am referring to our current theorizing about how the use of the analytic space as an extension of the maternal body container, which holds and gives coherence to the self, first makes symbolic thinking possible. This includes the less widely developed but important metaphor of breathing, which analysts influenced by Eastern thought have discussed (Eigen, 1993; Shapiro, 1996), to suggest how the body holds tension so that the mind is not overwhelmed by it.

The formulation of this aspect of the psychoanalytic process sprang from the observation that many people suffered from an inability to represent affect except through acting; they could not "use" the analyst (Winnicott, 1971), that is, the intersubjective properties of the relationship. Whereas Freud had articulated the means of interpreting unconscious symbolization, it now became necessary to theorize the conditions that foster development of symbolic capacity. We might see this as no longer taking dreaming, primary process, for granted, rather recognizing it as an accomplishment. Bion (1959, 1962), who took this crucial step beyond Freud, focused on thinking, the capacity for elaborating symbolic reality, as an achievement, distinguishing between thought that tolerates feeling and mere evacuating bad feeling into the other. While Bion formulated the maternal function that sponsors thinking as the container, Winnicott (1971) formulated along the lines of the intermediate space and the conditions of symbolic play. The person who remains unable to process bodily tension except through motoric discharge or somatic symptoms could be described not as lacking speech or symbolic capacity, but as lacking a *relationship* that is a condition of that capacity.

This relationship in which subjectivity develops is predicated on certain kinds of activity by the other. Psychoanalytic developmental theory has intensively explored various metaphors—containment, holding, recognition, affect attunement—for the maternal activity that is necessary to form the somatic sense of self and to perceive and think about the me and not-me environment; in other words, to become one's own container, able to own affects rather than be overwhelmed by them. The mother acts as an outside other who is able to help the subject to process and tolerate internal states of tension. The first form she assumes is that of concrete physical other, whose holding and breathing contain the child, whose nourishment stimulates and soothes. However, this concrete experience has formal elements—such as timing, kinetics, distance and closeness—that later enter into speech (Beebe & Lachmann, 1994) and so are already a basis for the subsequent metaphorical object of representation. The evolution from a concrete to a metaphorical experience is contingent on some achievement of bodily regulation and its intersubjective quality of recognition, through which the body metaphorically becomes the mental container. Therefore this container-body, for which the mother's body is the cultural/theoretical template, should not be dismissed into an unrepresentable presymbolic—as in Lacanian theory—but should in fact be seen as something that attains metaphoric dimensions and remains a substrate of affective life that is more or less in awareness.[4]

In sum, the early two-body experience is seen as crucial to the way that representation emerges intersubjectively; specifically, rep-

---

[4] Let me briefly allude to the debate among psychoanalytic feminists that hinges on this question. The idea that hysteria represents a return to the preoedipal relation to the mother, and thus a privileged feminine experience of access to the maternal body, a "concept of the feminine outside discourse" and a direct relation to the body outside language, is critiqued by Rose (1985). However the terms of this debate strike me as false. My point is that we see hysteria as symptomatic of failure in the relational conditions of bodily integration, which is in turn the precursor of speech and the basis for metaphorical, symbolic thinking, for speech's faculty of representation and communication. Hysteria is not a "return" to the maternal, in this view, for we do not agree that the maternal lies outside representation, nor that it can only be approached retroactively through the oedipal.

resentation is mediated through the evolution of the transitional space, which includes not only the fantasy experience of "alone-with-other" but also dialogic interaction. The transitional or potential space often has been noted as important between analyst and patient; but again, it should be observed in the alternations between reverie and two-person dialogue, not merely in the former. Language is the heir to the transitional space (Green 1986) inasmuch as we see it less in its Lacanian sense as subjecting the individual to the symbolic structure, and more relationally as forming the medium of the subject's acting on and interacting with the world. Hence it constitutes a space of fluctuating convergence and divergence between inner and outer. When we consider language as speech between subjects, we modify our understanding of the move from body to speech. Speech no longer figures as the activity of a subject empowered to speak, but as a possibility given by the relationship with a recognizing other. Or, we could say, speech is conditioned by the recognition between two subjects, rather than a property of the subject. Because communicative speech establishes a space of dialogue potentially outside the mental control of either or both participants, it is a site of mediation, the "third term."[5] Significantly, this understanding of intersubjectivity has grown from our attention to the analytic and maternal dyads.

In the dialogic structure, identification can evolve. Mediated by symbolic expression, identification can become not a collapse of differentiation, but a basis for understanding the position of the other. The kind of separation that allows this symbolic development is predicated not merely on a boundary set by an outside other (an abstract idea of limiting the omnipotent self) but rather on a maternal subjectivity that is able to represent affect and hence process the pain of separation between the mother and her child. This maternal

---

[5] I have argued elsewhere (Benjamin, 1995c) that we can set the dialogue of the maternal dyad in the place of Lacan's third term that breaks the dyad, the symbolic father or phallus. This is significant because Lacanian feminists such as Mitchell took this point to mean that there was no escape from the "dyadic trap" (Mitchell, 1974) other than the patriarchal form. Intersubjective space, I suggested (Benjamin, 1988) more broadly, could be understood in terms of the dialogue as creating a third, something like the dance that is distinct from the dancers yet cocreated by them. Ogden's (1995) idea of the analytic third is the most intense exposition of this idea of a cocreated yet independent relationship of two subjectivities.

subjectivity will be the object of the child's cross-identifications, as First (1988) shows, in the dialogic processing of loss, separation, aggression, indeed, negation in general.

This elaboration of the mother's mental work of representation or thinking (and *work*, as the nineteenth-century metaphor for transformations of energy, seems an appropriate term, as does Ruddick's [1989] *maternal thinking*) becomes an archimedean point of the shift in the notion of the subject as active representer of the world. We can recast Freud's original terms for attaining subjectivity and consider more closely what it means to work through the splitting between active and passive that has played such a role in psychoanalytic theory. The ability to represent and thereby regulate or digest bodily/affective stimuli and tension—which is indeed the primary work or activity of the psyche—may still be seen as the antidote or counterpole to passive subjection. But this ability is better understood as derivative of maternal thinking. Mothers' psychic work involves a response that unites the elements generally understood as passive—taking in—and active—giving back or putting out. The processing of other's psychic material, and its integration in intersubjective expression—recognition—constitutes the active-passive reconciliation in the work of the maternal subject.

Conceptually, this notion of recognition as activity indicates the basis for transcending the split complementarity in which the (traditionally female) other was, if not helplessly subjected to the subject's power, still relegated to the position of passivity in order to mirror his activity, contain his unmanageable tension. Providing mirroring and containment would, in effect, compromise her own subjectivity and disrupt her capacity for thinking (Brennan, 1992). Whereas in the intersubjective conception of recognition, two active subjects may exchange, may alternate in expressing and receiving, cocreating a mutuality that allows for and presumes separateness. The arena for this catching and throwing is the intermediate in-between space, the dialogue which becomes the "third term."

Historically, as long as the identificatory channel was blocked at the level of gender, as long as the intersubjective potential of the maternal dyad was insufficiently theorized, psychoanalytic theory could not really raise to the symbolic level this critique of complementarity. This insufficiency is intrinsically related to the inability to represent—in theory and in life—an identification with the mother as a subject: a desiring sexual subject, to be recognized as a person in her own right. In addition, it is related to a split in the female subject that divides her in two, inhabiting either the object position of feminine sexuality or the laboring position of maternal activity. As long as psychoanalysis could not theorize maternal psychic work as an aspect of subjectivity, it could not formulate a mother who is more than merely a mirror to the child's activity, or active otherwise than as an organizer of her child's experience. It could not evolve an idea of active femininity. Insofar as these divisions reflected the basic paradigm of subject and object, psychoanalysis remained captive to the active-passive binary in the analytic relationship.

Is it coincidental that, in the era that witnessed the feminist demand for equal, mutual participation by two subjects, the intersubjective perspective in psychoanalysis has developed? In a variety of ways feminist theory has discussed how the gender hierarchy has worked to obscure, to keep unrepresented, the already existing potential for mutual recognition in the maternal dyad. It has thus obscured the means by which split complementarity can be transformed through intersubjective representation of action and affect.

VII

In conclusion, I will briefly sketch how the prohibition on representing maternal identification perpetuates the active-passive complementarity so fateful for psychoanalysis. The child's attempt to reverse the complementarity against the mother—by actively discharging into a controlled container as well as by controlling her—is an important (and, again, probably inevitable) piece of mental life. What *is* problematic is the institutionalization of this reversal as the predominant form of masculine activity. In accord with other feminist thinkers (see Chodorow, 1979), I have theorized that this reversal is consolidated during the oedipal phase, when the boy repudiates the identification with the mother, thus losing access to an important means of remaining in relation to her (Benjamin, 1988; 1995c). This, in turn, makes more dangerous the now sexualized stimulation that, in his mind at least, appears not as his own desire but as emanating from her—all the more so, because he cannot identify with her as a container of his own feelings. The boy does not so much strive to contain as mother contains, but rather to project or split off the experience of being the passive, stimulated one—lodging this helplessness in the female and defining it as the feminine position. At the same time, the boy displaces the mother's envied activity onto the father with whom the boy identifies, rather than seeking to directly appropriate maternal activity as a form of power.

In the oedipal transformation, then, the aspect of passivity, which reflects the experience of being the helpless baby and the overstimulated oedipal child, devolves onto the feminine position: It becomes "feminine passivity." This position becomes the structural basis for the figure of the daughter, as reflected in Freud's oedipal theory of the girl's passive sexuality in relation to the father. This creation of a "feminine" representation, which transmutes the boy's own position of dependency and powerlessness, is precisely represented in his idea of the oedipal daughter's switch from being identified with the active mother to being the father's passive object (Benjamin, 1995c). (As Horney, 1926, contended, one could see the whole set of propositions about the female oedipus complex as mirroring the view of the oedipal boy.)

We might well say that the *Studies* provide an allegory of the way in which the daughter's position, the renunciation of activity and absorption in passivity, leads to the speechlessness, the *Unmundigkeit* of hysteria. Combined with the cultural prohibition on female aggression—cutting off recourse to any form of defensive activity, the well-known reversal out of passivity—this position makes hysteria the daughter's disease (Showalter, 1985). What is it in the daughter's passive position—the switch from mother to father—that dictates the form of her illness, even when the symptoms are not directly related to sexual passivity, to exploitation or sexual abuse?

Freud's awareness of and sympathy for the debilitating constraints in his patient's lives stands in striking contrast to his theorizing the daughter's sexually passive position in the Oedipus complex. A number of writers have posed the question, (see e.g. Sprengnether, 1990) What interfered with Freud's identification with the maternal? What made him insist so vociferously that Dora ought to have enjoyed Herr K.'s grabby seduction (Bernheimer & Kahane, 1985)? I would ask, what made him take up a position of split complementarity in relation to the feminine? It is not my aim here to speculate about Freud, but merely to offer a possible explanation for his theory of feminine passivity. In so doing I am implicitly suggesting a theory about the construction of femininity, one which overlaps in many essentials with ideas Brennan (1992) has formulated from a somewhat different perspective. The gist of my argument is that the oedipal switch to passivity be understood not as a product of the girl's search for the penis but of her compliance with the father's search for a passive object (a search which inspires the cultural norm of femininity)

Let us say that the male child's repudiation of his own passivity, associated with humiliation at the hands of the mother (she rejects him, leaves him, tantalizes him), sparks the father's fantasy of the daughter's passivity. Then consider Freud's train of thought when he asserts, in a paper concurrent with the *Studies*, the "Neuropsychoses of Defence," (1896) that a repressed feminine passivity lodges behind the male's obsessional use of defensive, aggressive activity. In other words, a certain kind of activity is necessary in order to overcome helplessness, and this kind of defensive activity structures the masculine position (Christiansen, 1993). If father-daughter incest represents the most egregious encapsulation of this defense, it is made possible by the generalized complementary relationship between the sexes, in which the daughter functions not merely as the split off embodiment of the passive object, but also the missing maternal container into whom the father discharges and expels unmanageable tension. The dual function of embodying passivity and containing unmanageable projected tension gives form to femininity; this femininity centers on the daughter, not the mother, as its defining figure. This structuring of the daughter position, seen as a product of the male oedipal transformation (its later retroactive *nachtraeglich* appearance in the father) may be the missing link in explaining the equation of hysteria with femininity.

At the same time, this structure suggests why the feminist might refuse love in favor of active mastery, or why the hysteric refuses sex: Because the daughter's position has entailed accepting the position of intolerable passivity (in order to be his desire, as she might earlier have tried to be her mother's desire). It is worth noting here that both Anna and Dora nursed their fathers through long illnesses, clung to and identified with them, incorporated their symptoms. They became containers for the other, but were unable to contain (lacked a maternal container) themselves.

I have suggested that we understand the active-passive gender complementarity as an oedipal form, not merely repudiating identification with feminine passivity but actually shaping it, in a reversal that negates the mother's activity. The masculine subjectivity that emerges from this move reflects both the absence of identification with a containing mother and the failure to represent the mother as a sexual subject. Irigaray (1991) has argued that, above all, it is the cultural failure to represent the umbilicus, which is both the link and the separation from mother, that sets up the phallus to represent what it does not (reunion/separation), making of it a defense. The use of the phallus to occlude the symbolic importance of the scar, the umbilicus, that should represent our loss of the mother actually produces what it defends against: the appearance of an unsymbolizable, overwhelming psychic experience. The inability to represent the mother underlies the confusion around activity and passivity that appears repeatedly in Freud's writings, and especially the misleading equation of phallic with active (as in "phallic mother"). What, if anything, would constitute femininity, if the split between maternal activity and the daughter's love of the father were transcended? How would psychoanalysis understand female oedipal, heterosexual love if it were not constituted by this split, and so no longer equated with passivity? These are questions I must leave for further speculation.

For the moment it must suffice to suggest what might be recovered and represented beyond the dominance of the active-passive complementarity. I have elaborated elsewhere (Benjamin, 1995b) how it is possible to theorize a different position in relation to gendered oppositions, formulate a different kind of complementarity than the one that emerges in the oedipal: that of have and have-not, phallus or no-phallus. To go beyond the polarization of the oedipal might mean to change the form of complementarity—perhaps a parallel move to the way that sustaining identification with different positions transforms complementarity in the countertransference.

While in the oedipal phase the child understands the mutual exclusivity of the gender polarity to mean, "If I try to have what the other has, I will lose what I have," in the postoedipal complementarity, one can tolerate the tension of opposing desires and identifications. In effect, accepting the very incompleteness of each position makes multiple positions possible: not precisely identifying with all positions at once, but aware of their possibility. This awareness allows a fuller symbolization, one that operates in the transitional area, bridging rather than splitting opposites such as active and passive (Bassin, 1997; Freedman, 1980). From this standpoint, true activity does not take the defensive form of repudiating passivity. Activity predicated on the activity-passivity split, directed toward a passive object, is merely action; it lacks the intersubjective space of a potential other. Such space, as we have seen, is the very condition of symbolic activity; in other words, the condition of the representational activity of the subject is always a representation of the other subject (which need not be a real other, and could be nothing less than the world outside). Characteristically, such activity can embrace receptivity to that other, responsive recognition of the other's impact on the self, and hence participation in the reality of two subjects. Of course, every psychoanalytic relationship has to work through oscillations between action and activity, split complementarity and mutuality, and so we are always rededicating ourselves to finding a path toward intersubjective speech.

Insofar as defensive repudiation of passivity helped to constitute the figure of ideal mastery that has burdened psychoanalysis, psychoanalysis must go beyond the oedipal complementarity to cure itself. The characteristic of the postoedipal complementarity is that it can hold paradoxical rather than oppositional formulations. It is this that gives rise to a third position that neither denies nor splits difference, but holds it in paradoxical state of being antagonistic and reconcilable at once. This is the position that can tolerate the incessant reversals of opposites by weaving from the attraction to both sides a net. A net that allows us to take the primal leap of psychoanalysis, the leap into the space between certain knowledge and unthinking action, the space of negative capability that is thought.

To become disinvested in any one position, in this way, is close to the goal of mental freedom that Freud strove to formulate. To even imagine such freedom, Freud knew, requires a consciousness of our own investment; what we have added, perhaps, is that this is only possible by becoming aware of our inevitable participation in the split complementarities that organize our lives and our thought. Thus, the reintegration of the missing half of the complementarity is always a necessary step to thinking through that splitting. Toward this end, I have called upon the figure of Anna/Bertha, alongside the figure of Freud, so that our imagination will continue to include whoever, whatever, appears in the guise of the complementary other and so that we may view afresh the reversal between analyst and analyzed. Such reversals mark the dialogic encounter with those others, which is at the heart of the psychoanalytic endeavor, calling forth our own reaction to the action of the other, whose pain, passion and opposition will inevitably unclothe us to ourselves, and tell us, Think again!

2

"Constructions of Uncertain Content"

Gender and Subjectivity beyond the Oedipal Complementarities

> Even in the sphere of human sexual life you soon see how inade-
> quate it is to make masculine behavior coincide with activity and
> feminine with passivity. A mother is active in every sense towards
> her child. . . . One might consider characterizing femininity psy-
> chologically as giving preference to passive aims. This is not,
> of course, the same thing as passivity; to achieve a passive aim
> may call for a large amount of activity. . . . The suppression of
> women's aggressiveness which is prescribed for them constitu-
> tionally and imposed on them socially favors the development of
> powerful masochistic impulses . . . binding erotically the destruc-
> tive trends, which have been diverted inwards. Thus masochism,
> as people say, is truly feminine.
>
> —Freud, 1933

> [A]ll human individuals, as a result of their bisexual disposition
> and of cross-inheritance, combine in themselves both masculine
> and feminine characteristics, so that pure masculinity and femi-
> ninity remain theoretical constructions of uncertain content.
>
> —Freud, 1925

The Phenomenology of Gender Categories

I open this text with Freud's well-known comments on feminine passivity, with the expectation that something new can be gained from
examining yet again the contradictions that arise in them. This might
appear a vain hope, so often have these remarks been the subject of
critical inquiry. Still, at the very least, I believe they may serve to reveal some of the most important questions of gender. In recent years

we—and here I mean we in a quite literal sense, speaking of my generation of feminists, psychoanalysts as well as theorists who have combined those two approaches—have had the opportunity to reexperience, as Freud did, that we are bound to falter if we try to address the question of gender by asking, What are masculinity and femininity? If we have come to see that it is as difficult to formulate the question as it is to advance an answer, still, we have made considerable headway in eliminating certain questions and answers. We have come to accept the paradoxical status of gender categories, such that they at once fit and contradict our experience, both appear derived from reality and yet spring from the shifting ground of fantasy.

The most militant contemporary critique of the assumptions underlying the original psychoanalytic treatment of gender and sexuality has been articulated in postmodern/poststructural feminist thought (for discussions see Braidotti, 1991; Butler, 1990; Fuss, 1989; Harraway, 1988; Nicholson, 1990). Much recent psychoanalytic work on gender (Benjamin, 1995b; Dimen, 1991, 1995; Gerson, 1996b; Goldner, 1991; Harris, 1991; S. Mitchell, 1996b) claims to be influenced by this critique. In the poststructural position elaborated by Moi (1985b), and French criticism, Butler (1990) in particular, we find not only a rejection of biological, transhistorical foundations of sexuality and gender, which have been used to legitimate masculine power claims; but also objection to the idea of gender identity as a coherent, seamless, reified entity—even when it takes the form of feminist appeals to a naturalized feminine identity or a specific feminine difference. (Butler has French writers in mind but certainly this would include American tropes such as "a different voice," (Gilligan, 1982) "women's ways of knowing," (Belenky et al. 1986) or woman's relational self (Jordan, 1992)). For any such fixing of feminine identity would serve to reaffirm woman's location within the terms of the binary opposition man-woman and so reinstall hierarchical gender categories as if they were simply pregiven, created in nature. Deconstructionist thought has itself not been exempt from this scrutiny of the effects of using woman's standpoint as a basis for criticism. Rose (1986) contends that the interrogation of the masculine subject from the standpoint of its excluded other, Woman, restabilizes woman's "classic position of otherness" and perpetuates "the constant identification of the woman with the underside of truth."

The idea informing this critique is that rather than take sides in the controversy between nature and culture, the social and the biological, one should recognize those oppositions themselves as constructions, artifice (Brennan, 1989, 1992). The postmodern feminist position thus differs from those that reassert women's feminine difference as well as from de Beauvoir's earlier rejection of feminine "immanence" as a product of male domination (Butler, 1990): Its focus is not simply on woman's position as Other to the male subject, but on the binary logic that produces the complementarity male subject–female object (as in Irigaray, 1985, 1991). On the other hand, if we do not begin with the opposition between woman and man, with woman's negative position in that binary, we seem to dissolve the very basis for our having questioned gender categories in the first place.

The critique of gender complementarity results in a necessary paradox: It at once upsets the oppositional categories of femininity and masculinity while recognizing that these positions inescapably organize experience (Dimen, 1991), remaining operative as "real appearances" (Benjamin, 1992, citing Marx). As Harris (1991) has expressed it, gender is "neither reified nor simply liminal and evanescent. Rather, in any one person's experience, gender may occupy both positions. Gender may in some contexts be thick and reified . . . at other moments, gender may seem porous and insubstantial" (p. 212). In a closely related statement, Dimen (1991) maintained that this elusiveness should not "be regarded as a failure of method or theory. Instead, it is a *sign* of what gender is" (p. 349).

It follows that the continued dissolution and resurrection of gender as a binary may well be—in our culture, at least—its primary determination. If carried to its most radical conclusion, does such thinking do away with the question of sexual difference? Not exactly. But having established that gender works in us not through something as stable or coherent as an identity, may change the question. What happens when the concept of identity is seen as abrogated or, more modestly, balanced by multiplicity (Aron, 1996), when we understand people to have shifting, conflicting gender identifications (one moment I am mother's reparative daughter, then I am father's ambitious son)? Does the idea of multiplicity overthrow the original psychoanalytic framework of two sexes poised in different relationships to one organ, the phallus?

This is an important question because even recently some feminist psychoanalytic thinkers have retained this phallic framework. The division that began with Freud's (e.g. 1925) idea of sexual difference centered around the castration complex—having or not having the phallus—is one that Lacanian feminists have continued to make central to their thought, albeit in the modified form of "having or being" the phallus (see Mitchell, 1982; Rose, 1982). They have argued that there is no other position from which to explain sexual difference and heterosexuality as a psychic reality, to lift them out of the realm of the natural, which requires no explanation. Is this so? Or is the pursuit of such an explanation itself problematic? I shall address these issues in the course of this essay.

To begin, however, let us focus on the paradox mentioned earlier. Let us say that the binary gender categories are analytically necessary to explain deeply embedded psychic experience, but what fundamental reality they refer to remains unclear; it need not be characterized in terms of singular, distinct identities or positions. Since gender is necessarily indeterminate, Goldner (1991) has proposed, it presents psychoanalysis with an "epistemological paradox." We "might think of gender as a transcendent analytic category whose truth, though false, remains central to thought; indeed, it constructs the very analytic categories we would use to *de*construct it . . ." (p. 256). To use this paradoxical "false truth" of gender, I suggest, we should understand the binary opposition of masculine-feminine as a superordinate logic; that is, it transcends any concrete relationship, any concrete determinations or characteristics. For concrete relationships necessarily alter and explode, even as they use and express, the abstract polarities of gender. In psychic reality, the phenomenal stuff of relationships is inflected by or placed in reference to such oppositional forms, or marked by its divergence from them. I will be arguing that the continued use of these categories to construct and deconstruct the relationships in which gender appears to us also requires a kind of reconstruction, in the original psychoanalytic sense of that term: an interpretation that specifies their origins in a psychic complex, in the psychosexual history of the individual—a culturally situated individual.

As we see in the quotations above, in Freud's work the oscillation between construction and deconstruction of gender categories is already observable, though not self-consciously noted. Thus, he repeatedly makes use of and rejects the constructions of activity and passivity to define masculinity and femininity. The reconstructive interpretation of this crucial contradiction in Freud will lead us to an examination of the subject-object complementarity in its relation to the Oedipus complex. It will allow us to analyze more deeply the heterosexual structure, so long accepted by psychoanalysis, in which the position of woman is that of object to a presumed male subject.

Some Psychic Consequences of
the Subject-Object Logic

Let us begin by considering our view of the term *subject*, a term that unavoidably calls to mind far-flung debates we shall not consider. What we are really interested in here is the idea of subjectivity.[1] Implicit in the idea of subjectivity, as I see it, is not only the idea of agency—the activity that Freud repeatedly associated with the masculine—but also authorship (Benjamin, 1988). And here we may note an important distinction between activity paired with its opposite, passivity, and activity that includes authorship, or ownership. The significance of this distinction becomes apparent in discussions of subjectivity by contemporary theorists. Quite divergent thinkers from traditions such as contemporary Kleinian theory and self psychology have arrived at the intersubjectively conceived self, characterized by what I call authorship (Benjamin, 1988)—the condition of ownership that reflects intentionality and bestows the awareness of others states, feelings, and intentions. For instance, Ogden (1986) contrasts the depressive sense of the self as "I" with the paranoid-schizoid sense of "itness," the raw experience of "feeling is happening." By subjectivity we seem to mean a continuity of consciousness that mediates between the experience or feeling and its meaning or object, at once giving it a context and creating a space between self and object. Then again Stern (1985) proposes that the subjective self refers to a sense of having an interior experience, knowing that others have it too, and the possibility of sharing it. Already, in the evocation of interiority and space, we have an intuition of something that cannot be resolved back into the terms of activity contrasted to passivity.

Briefly, let me sum up my thesis. As psychoanalysis moves from its original subject-object paradigm to an intersubjective one, we subtly change the meaning of activity; we conceive it in the context not of a polar complementarity but of a symmetry between two

---

[1] These remarks were organized for a comment on a paper by Leon Hoffman (1996) contending that Freud's inability to recognize woman's subjectivity was at the heart of his problematic assumptions about femininity. Hoffman defined subjectivity as the capacity to posit the self as the independent agent who determines or controls thoughts and actions. To integrate woman's subjectivity would, Hoffman contended, extend to women aspects of psychic life that received short shrift in Freud's thinking about femininity, e.g. aggression and sexual desire and above all entitlement to the active position.

active partners. And this allows a reconfiguration of terms: However uncertain their contents, masculinity and femininity are no longer in the same formal relation to each other, separated by an uncrossable, fixed divide. Within the subject-object paradigm, in which there is always one subject, never two, it is necessary that whatever one side gains the other must lose. In that formal structure the Other, let us say woman, could only become subject by reversal, by displacing man into the position of object, which would hardly have been acceptable. In a sense, the idea of subjectivity could not be extended to women within the subject-object paradigm because only reversal, not extension of the subject position was possible. In that construction, activity had to be subtracted from femininity or inevitably passivity would devolve onto the masculine.

The polarity *activity-passivity* was the most salient example of this formal principle in Freud's writing; it was the construction he made central to gender, which he both repeatedly referred to and questioned. (This does not mean that he never understood woman to be a subject. In Freud's usage a girl takes her father as object while fulfilling a passive aim. However, while she is technically the subject, her femininity is set up as the passive counterpart of masculine activity.) Significantly, the active-passive antinomy turns back upon itself, much as the constructs of gender do. It is apt to break down, as when Freud (1933) wonders who is to be called active in the mother-baby relation—the mother suckling or the baby sucking. Yet it is continually reestablished, as when he says a bit further on that the abandonment of the clitoris "clears the phallic activity out of the way, smooths the ground for femininity," (128) or that the girl's play with dolls is "not in fact an expression of her femininity; it served as an identification with her mother with the intention of substituting activity for passivity" (128). This activity is what she must give up to assume the feminine position.[2] Thus, no sooner does Freud doubt the equation of femininity with passivity

---

[2] Notice that this manner in which the girl's passivity evolves in the "Femininity" essay follows the same movement as in Freud's (1915a) elucidation of sadomasochism in "Instincts and their Vicissitudes," though in reverse— there, a primary sadism, aggression actually, is turned inward to masochism, and then back outward to intentional sadism. Here a primary passivity at the hands of the mother is turned around to an active position to do to self or other what was done to her, and then once again reverts to passivity in relation to the father.

than he reestablishes it, insisting that it is not the identification with mother but the oedipal turn to the father as love object that makes the girl truly feminine.

Let us now take a closer look at the grounding of masculine and feminine positions in the deep structure of the subject-object complementarity established in the oedipal. Let us consider Freud's taxonomy of love in his 1914 essay "On Narcissism," in which the same unwinding and rewinding of gender logic prevail as in the later problematic remarks on femininity. As you know, Freud here asserts "fundamental differences" between "male and female sexes . . . in respect of their type of object-choice" (88). He defines in contrast to narcissism the object love of the anaclitic type (leaning on the ego instincts—loving the one who feeds, cares for, and protects you). Such object love is characteristic only of the man who loves women. Women, beautiful ones anyway—and here he has "no tendentious desire to depreciate women," he assures us—seemingly only wish to be loved. Indeed, they become the object of the man's "sexual overvaluation" for those who have renounced such narcissism themselves are fascinated by those who retain that child-like "self-contentment and inaccessibility" (88). But does this not suggest that object love derives from renounced narcissism?

So, we may presume, women now take up the place of the child adored by the mother, or (as in Freud's famous statement at the end of the passage) of "His Majesty the Baby," loved by the parents who vicariously fulfill their own narcissism. In other words, the passive female love object is actually like the narcissistic child, who is self-contented and unconcerned, blissfully unaware of dependency or anaclasis—of course because, we must add, they are adored by mother. Oddly, it seems that women themselves generally only direct this adoration toward their children—except insofar as they fall into ideal love of their masculine selves, represented by grown men they would wish to be, thus making "the step in development from narcissism to object love" (90).

Here Freud clearly acknowledges the homoerotic identificatory basis for women's active love, but again, this love does not count as feminine. Inasmuch as Freud goes on to show how all falling in love reflects a projection of our ideal, the part our ego cannot realize, it might seem that both sexes might engage the other as the lost ideal of their masculine or feminine self. But not only would this realization establish the symmetry of two subjectivities, it would also reveal the feminine identification of the man in his activity of loving: Like the

41

woman who projects her own "boyish nature" into the man she loves, the man would be projecting his feminine self.

The basic structural relation of narcissism and love is represented by Freud in his establishment of the original mother-son couple, the boy who loves the woman who cares for him, and the woman who adoringly, narcissistically loves this boy. From this representation arises a mass of contradictions. Since love is expressed in couplets of lover and loved, never mutual, we do not see the boy adoring his mother, only loving anaclitically. Yet, when he becomes a man does he in fact love anaclitically? Or doesn't he rather reverse maternal narcissism, representing his child self in the self-contained beautiful woman whom he adores, unreciprocated, as his mother loved him? What Freud calls "the step from narcissism to object-love" has seemingly little to do with anaclisis—loving the one who feeds or protects you. Rather, it reflects the reversal of narcissism, placing the woman in the role of the adored child. The man's overvaluing love of the narcissistic woman seems hardly different from Freud's depiction of the male homosexual's love for someone who represents his child self, except that in this case Freud can recognize the man's identification with maternal narcissism. If Freud, in a blatant contradiction, calls the masculine heterosexual form of adoration the one completely anaclitic love, the one love which is not narcissistic, is it because of his persistent blind spot regarding male identification with women?

Further difficulties arise from the subject-object structure in the original couple. Who is the subject here, the boy who is beloved, or the mother who actively loves him? Freud's description ignores the possibility of anaclitic love, dependency, in which the child actively reciprocally loves, rather than being the mere object of the mother's nurturing activity. It misses the possibility of a mutual adoration, in which the mother is actually the boy's ideal, as well as he hers. Then again, his notion of the self-contained woman reflects an image of the self-sufficient (preoedipal) breast-mother who seems to need no one. Only the man needs the woman, and his need becomes his love. I believe we can see here the difficulty that arises because Freud is captive to the logic of only one subject, only one active lover, never two. This allows only reversal of complementarity but not a transformation into mutuality. Intrinsically linked to this logic is the necessity of saving the active position for the adult male, the passive one for his beloved. Perhaps the threatening aspect of identifying with woman lies in the fact that in Freud's mind, already and finally, the feminine is, despite all denials, ineluctably allied with passivity, is necessarily defined by a perverse complementarity of subject and object?

It is difficult to express this psychic constellation in causal terms. Perhaps it will suffice to say that the formal logic of complementarity, which insists on reversal, is hooked up with the specific aim of resisting passivity and lodging it in the feminine. On one hand, the insistence that woman's aggression be directed inward, take a passive aim, suggests the fear of the reversal inherent in the structure of the subject-object complementarity. If women were sexually aggressive, then men would be the object of that putatively devouring, rapacious passion. Neither women nor men want to own this possibility. In view of the necessary fusion of aggression with sexuality, woman's aggression must take the form of masochism, which by this complementary logic must be feminine. On the other hand, perhaps the complementary form itself expresses this deepest fear: that the primary other, the mother, could be greedy, dangerous, violent. In the position formed around this fear, the infantile self remains lodged in a paranoid stance toward the other, in which her existence as a subject could only mean suppression of ours. A conception of another stance for the subject, as in Klein's depressive position or constituted in the terms of intersubjectivity, is required to step out of this zero-sum relationship (Benjamin, 1995c): a subject who can achieve a mediating space between the symbol and the thing, a sense of ownership of its own acts and meanings, and therefore escapes this cycle of doer and done to. But Freud's notions of femininity and masculinity, of narcissism and object love, seem utterly imbued with this logic of the One and the Other. They testify to the historically pervasive form of subjectivity which has evolved in relation to a subordinated, excluded other.

The Question of Sexual Difference

Here we must take up the question that has, since the seminal statements by Mitchell (1974) and Chodorow (1978) in the seventies, divided Object Relations and Lacanian feminist thinkers: the question of whether to analyze the gender divide in terms of the structural relationship to the phallus, or of the object relation to the mother (see Brennan, 1989). I will ultimately propose transcending this dispute because I believe that a reconstructive analysis of the oedipal position offers another angle on the constitution of sexual difference, albeit perhaps a less centered explanation. Even as we are able to critique the subject-object complementarity from the standpoint of the subject-subject relation (intersubjectivity), so we are able to critique the oedipal position from the standpoint of the postoedipal recuperation of overinclusiveness. In subsequent sections I will make a case that oedipal gender complementarity, which has dominated psychoanalysis, is not the only psychic formation that contributes to sexual subjectivity; indeed, that its dominance is based on the suppression of another psychic formation that we also observe in a reality messier and more various, which shapes our relationships and contributes to our creativity as well as our ability to subvert the binary system. But first, let us clarify the terms of the dispute.

While critics of object relations theory have claimed that the emphasis on the preoedipal formation in women has led to a deracinated view of women's sexuality and aggression, in fact this tendency began with Freud's own construction of woman's oedipal situation, which excluded from femininity both the jealous wish to be like mother and the active desire for the father (see Horney, 1924); only the narcissistic injury of castration and its compensation, the passive wish for the father, were truly feminine. The legacy of Freud's position was a splitting between oedipal and preoedipal along the gender divide. Often these positions were aligned with paternal (phallic) and maternal (holding) stances in the analyst. It may be that the initial splitting can be traced back to Freud's double difficulty with femininity: with recognizing the boy's preoedipal identifications with the mother as well as the girl's ability to be an active subject who owns a desire for her father not narcissistically mediated by penis envy.

As is well known, the narcissism of the feminine position consisted not only in woman's wish to be loved. The pivotal thesis around which Freud elaborates sexual difference is the idea of castration: the realization that women do not have the penis. This affects each sex differently and thereby accounts for the difference between them: Boys wish to protect their narcissistic possession and so give up their oedipal wish for the mother; girls recognize their lack and turn away from the mother and toward the father who can give them the penis in the familiar equation penis=baby. However, Freud acknowledged that this circuitous route to what he called femininity was a difficult one, likely to fail, and leave the girl stranded in the "masculinity complex," refusing to give up the pre-oedipal relation to mother or the identification with the male position, continuing to envy the penis.

This basic set of premises was defended by Mitchell (1974) from a feminist Lacanian standpoint as a way of explaining sexual difference and domination, but was criticized by Chodorow (1978) who stressed the girl's sense of continuity with her mother and her use of the father to separate. Chodorow argued that the mother's unconscious identification with her daughter contrasted with her positioning of her son as complementary other, thus establishing a foundation for the girl's greater preoccupation with preoedipal issues of separation and the boy's tendency to make his sexual difference the basis of separateness. Thus Chodorow makes women's mothering the pivotal point of departure for explaining the respective positions taken up by boys as mother's complementary object and girls as mother's self-reflection. The question of separation becomes more central to understanding psychic reality, and the feminine sense of self appears less as lack and more as continuity with the maternal object.

According to Mitchell (1982), and others who share her Lacanian perspective such as Adams (1982) and Rose (1982), the essential problem with Chodorow's object relations position is that it relies on a preexisting notion of gender complementarity, assuming rather than trying to explain the origins of sexual difference. In this view, Chodorow merely shows how mothers pass on an already given difference. Sexual difference is no longer seen as fundamental to the constitution of the subject, and the social fact of women's universal role as mothers substitutes for psychic relations. Identity is seen as founded in identification with social roles, bypassing the incoherence of the unconscious and the fundamental role of absence in creating desire, hence sexuality. Heterosexuality is taken for granted rather than explained. It is not referred to the psychic reality of the castration complex. When the step of the castration complex is left out, it appears that identification causes sexual difference, while after all identification can only follow upon an already existing difference. As Adams (1982) states, Chodorow's thesis about gender development and her conclusion that shared parenting could overturn the gender system represent "the abolition of masculinity and femininity as traditionally understood. The psychoanalytic explanation of sexual difference has completely collapsed" (50).

Apart from the inaccuracy of this take on Chodorow, I think there are important reasons why this explanation (Freud's or Lacan's version) had to collapse, even though it may well be true that there are drawbacks to its alternative. It is possible to read against the grain Mitchell's remark that the object relations emphasis on the early maternal relation left the "problem of sexual distinction as a subsidiary that is somehow not bound up with the very formation of the subject. This is the price paid for the reorientation to the mother, and the neglect of the father" (22). I would venture to say that, as may be true with all reversals, for a time it was a price worth paying. If the focus on the preoedipal allowed the early relation to the mother to come into view, and if that amounted to a tilt away from the father, it is surely now being corrected. As I have shown, it is certainly possible to encompass the father in a focus on earlier separation-individuation (Benjamin 1986a, b; 1988; 1991). It may be that in order to emphasize the formation of the subject along the axes of good and bad, attachment and loss, self-other differentiation (as we see variously in Klein, Fairbairn, Winnicott, Bowlby, Mahler, Stern, to name only a few) it was necessary to move out of the range of the castration complex and its focus on the structure of sexual difference. It may be that these axes are just as or more fundamental than our sense of gendered self although inflecting it and inflected by it. Clinically, this approach to gender has been extremely fruitful, as, for instance, with Coates's (Coates, Friedman & Wolfe, 1991) understanding of how a preoedipal boy shifts his gender identification to feminine as a melancholic response to mother's depressed withdrawal. The emphasis on identifications has provided a basis for understanding such interplays between gender, separation, and loss.

So while it is true that such explanations partly depend upon the social reality of "who [in the family] is there to turn to," as Adams (1982) puts it, the structural underpinning of this position is not just social identification but a theory of separation-individuation. The psychic reality remains pivotal along the axes of loss and separation, identification and object love. These axes formulate a psychic reality which is by no means merely dependent on the social, and from that standpoint pursue the matter of gender. But precisely because of its plural, decentered focus on affective experience, that pursuit may not embrace a central explanation of sexual difference. And while early object relations theory certainly leaned upon unquestioned categories of masculinity and femininity, the recent work of relational analysts, as I have already stressed, has worked to challenge them. The focus on preoedipal experience, as we shall see later, also permitted the development of a conception of the psychic experience of gender that is contingent upon other configurations than the oedipal.

But let us now consider for a moment the opposition reflected in Mitchell's critique between a mother-centered and father-centered theory. I would ask, did not the opposition between mother and father begin with Freud's idea of the girl's oedipal switch? While Freud emphasized the little girl's preoedipal attachment to the mother, he continually asserted that this attachment was masculine (she is a "little man") and thus essentially heterosexual, phallic, masculine (even though, ironically, its object, the mother, is also not feminine). He asserted that her (oedipal) femininity could not be derived from her sense of likeness with her mother, because this after all entailed an identification with the active position. Thus, contrary to his own (1931) observation that little girls' doll play is a sign of their femininity before the castration complex—an observation that has been amplified by all subsequent dissenters from Freud—femininity has to be constituted specifically in relation to the father and phallus (Freud, 1933). Naturally, this raises the question as to why it is this, precisely, that is feminine—and Freud (1933) himself admits to being no less puzzled by it, referring his audience finally to the riddle of femininity and advising them to ask the poets.

Freud's own uncertainty, the puzzlement into which his observations about femininity and passivity lead, might well be taken to justify the idea of paradoxical gender, the proposition that the divide between masculinity and femininity is as contradictory and shifting as it is constant (Harris, 1991). But in a response to Dimen's (1991) elucidation of that proposition, Mitchell (1991) argues that such paradox is only phenomenological, experiential—it does not affect the ontological status of Freud's construction of a "theory as to how the meaning of the difference between the sexes is established in the mind" (354). I would agree with her that we seem to be working from two different epistemological positions here, one aiming for a centered ontology of the psychic origins of sexual difference, in which subjectivity is constituted through a single major division; the other aiming for a decentered phenomenology of the psychic, in which subjectivity emerges through shifting, multiple identifications that refer to an inconsistent though pervasive binary. In my view the Lacanian position, despite its emphasis on the split subject and the incoherent unconscious (Rose,

1982), restores in theory the very binary logic of identity that it subtracts from the subject: If the law "decenters and divides," (Mitchell, 1982) still the law is One.

I do, however, acknowledge the problems identified by Mitchell and Rose, even as I dispute their solution. Mitchell (1974; 1982) argued convincingly that early objections to Freud took gender difference for granted, and thus relegated it to nature. Chodorow agreed with Mitchell that those like Horney and Klein who dissented from Freud on the matter of penis envy did assume a natural heterosexuality, in Klein's case anchored in anatomy; both tended to overshoot psychic reality and anchor theory in the biological or social reality. It also may be true that theories beginning with the child's relation to mother only presume rather than explain the system of heterosexual complementarity, but is this avoidable? Is it necessary or even possible to postulate an archimedean point of leverage that does explain sexual difference? Does the insistence on this postulate really serve as a guarantee that we have kept our sights on psychic reality, or does it simply create another blind spot, another unacknowledged dependency upon the social or biological domain? Might not the demand for such a central structuring principle have to be suspended or, for that matter, analysed?

I will suggest that an equally problematic dependency underlies Mitchell's (1982) effort to explain sexual difference by reference to castration. The problem is that "the mark that distinguishes boys and girls," may not really be detached from a pregiven social or biological reality, as she seems to think it is. Mitchell asks "if castration is only one among other separations . . . then what distinguishes the two sexes?"(19) But here she is overtaken by the uncertainty of contents, for of what does the distinction between boys and girls, the "mark," consist? Mitchell seeks an answer by returning to Freud's contention that we must find "something that is specific for girls," something that explains "the termination of the attachment of girls to their mother . . . the castration complex" (Freud, 1933, 124). The distinction we are seeking, then, consists of the change in the love object: This move from mother to father defines the passage from the "masculine phase to the feminine one" (119). Mitchell appears to accept the idea that the sexual differentiation that constitutes the subject consists of the girl's oedipal turn, that sexual difference equals heterosexuality. And indeed, she (Mitchell, 1991) later states quite baldly that "Sexuality is the process that enables one to find the gendered other as different from oneself so that she or he can be used as other for the purpose of engendering" (355). One becomes gendered, in other words, through assuming the role of complementary opposite, the Other of the other. It turns out, then, that the riddle of femininity and the question of sexual difference have the same answer: Femininity consists of loving the father; *sexual difference is heterosexual orientation.*

Now we know that this understanding of sexual difference is precisely one that Freud (1920) continually challenges, as when he stated that "the literature of homosexuality usually fails to distinguish clearly enough between the questions of the choice of object ... and the sexual characteristics and sexual attitude of the subject ... as though the answer to the former necessarily involved answers to the latter. . . ." Still, we observe that in the very moment of asserting this ambiguity, Freud slips again into the language of gender contents, for he continues: "A man in whose character feminine attributes obviously predominate, who may, indeed, behave in love like a woman, . . . may nevertheless be heterosexual" (170).[3] Once again, we must wonder, of what do these feminine attributes and behavior consist? Perhaps, as Chodorow suggests, femininity is that identification with mother's part in the mother-baby dyad which keeps alive the forms of exchange, empathy and accommodation to other's needs we associate with mothering. If not, what is the "mark of difference"? Are we back to the notion of passivity? Or does it, indeed, consist of loving the father the way a daughter does?

Let us consider the odd premise at work: It is always only female sexuality that sets up the question of sexual difference. That is, in both Freud's and Mitchell's story, *boys' heterosexual orientation seems not to require explanation.* In fact, it is already there as a precondition of their castration complex, whose main import is to renounce that sexual desire. The boy's love of the mother predates and sets it

---

[3] Chodorow (1994) rightly cites this passage to illustrate the difference between gender and sexual object choice, a difference Mitchell (1991) disputes. Precisely this conflation of object choice with masculine or feminine identifications is what Chodorow overturned, by showing that preoedipal differences *precede* oedipal, heterosexual object choice. But, of course, the point is that Freud cannot hold to this position; when he seeks his explanation for the girl's femininity he lapses into a conflation of it with her heterosexual orientation. Again, we must ask, is it because of his strenuous refusal to see her identification with mother as feminine?

in motion: His relation to the mother is, in effect, a "natural" starting point. It is hard to see how this view of sexual difference is any less dependent upon the assumption of social or biological facts, regarding both heterosexuality and woman's mothering. I cannot see that Freud's view of the castration complex has explained how the boy's heterosexual structure has come into being; it has only shown why the little girl, for whom it is not "natural," who may even resist it, finally accedes to it. It must be, then, that the heterosexual structure brings about the castration complex, rather than being its result. Heterosexual orientation, which is purportedly the content of sexual difference, has not been explained at all.

It is certainly possible to begin with a social organization of heterosexuality and from this derive the psychic workings of heterosexuality, still incorporating the idea of castration. Rubin (1975) did this most persuasively, locating the phallus in its role as guaranteeing the exchange of women by men. She argued that the little girl gives up her love for the mother because she discovers that, having no phallus to exchange, she cannot have mother. For Rubin this explanation does not, as Mitchell would have it, refer to a resignation to "biological inadequacy" but to compliance with social organization: The prior taboo on homosexuality and the rule that women can only be exchanged against the phallus is what necessitates the girl's disappointment. Not surprisingly, those who reject the normatively natural status of the heterosexual structure but recognize it as a social given—object relations analysts like Stoller (1973) and Chodorow (1992)—have interrogated boys' accession to it as well. Stoller (1973) first argued that the boy's early relation to the mother was identificatory rather than heterosexual, and that boys' heterosexuality could only develop when preceded by a complicated process of disidentification and separation. Chodorow (1978) sought to show how the mother's unconscious fantasy helps effect this disidentification by conceiving the boy as her complementary other, her love object. Here the boy must move from a primary identification with his mother, not a heterosexual relationship to her.

Now this narrative about the boy might follow the same steps, applying to the boy the same logic Freud developed regarding the girl's renunciation of masculinity. The major question would be, how does the boy come to take his mother as love object and give up his "femininity complex." (See Chodorow, 1992; Lewes, 1988; Fast, 1984.) In this case masculinity would be as much a riddle as femininity.[4] Indeed, Chodorow suggests that the boy first defines himself as not-mother before, in the oedipal power move, he defines her as not-male, not the generic universal human he at first thought her to be (1980). Freud's premises have been reversed, highlighting identification as the primary bond, object love as a sequel. However, what this reversal points to is the binary logic, which has not been transcended, but remains central to either position, the maternal relational thesis or the father/phallus thesis. (This is doubtless why Chodorow, 1994, has more recently argued in favor of multiple positions that vary and diverge from the binary.) In the reversal, object love and identification still appear in a relation of mutual exclusivity. In this case the sexual divide has no content but the mutually negating principle, X is not-Y, Y is not-X. Both Freud's theory of the castration complex and the counterargument reveal the Oedipus complex to be a confrontation with the heterosexual imperative: the insistence that being and having, identification and object love must be split.

For Lacan, this split between identification and object love continues to be central to the understanding of how the boy becomes a subject, although elaborated somewhat differently. The separation from an imaginary omnipotent mother actually holds a parallel place to that in some object relations theory; separation figures as a precondition of male desire, of the heterosexual subject. Castration in this way does not mean simply the prohibition of a naturally assumed heterosexual desire, rather desire for the mother results from castration—the mother's castration, that is. In order to emerge from the imaginary world of omnipotent fantasy, the boy must come to see that mother is not self-sufficient and complete, does not have the phallus (or father's penis inside her, as Klein sees it), and so requires someone else to complete her (Lacan, 1977b)—she becomes "feminine." He must simultaneously recognize her and his own lack, represented by her desire for the phallus. He cannot both be her (be the

---

[4] In my earlier work, I also stressed this disidentification, although I later came to note that it is an oedipal phenomenon and, as Fast (1984) emphasized, preceded by a very strong identification with the mother and her reproductive capacities. Chodorow, I think, assumes too readily that this identification with mother is usually completely suppressed by paternal, masculine orientation rather than anchoring the boy's ability to mother in his over-inclusive identification with mother that can persist alongside the oedipal and often does.

phallus) and have her (have the phallus that reunites with her). The short answer to the question of sexual difference would then be: it consists only of the necessity of choice. The Oedipus complex poses for each child the necessity of choosing to be one thing and have the other, to identify on one side and love on the other.

This is a compelling way of understanding sexual difference, such that it requires no determinacy of contents. (Except, of course, the repeatedly asked question, Doesn't the phallus proposed here really mean the penis, a reinstitution of anatomic destiny? But "we let that pass, we do not press the point.") Does it, then, avoid the pitfalls of Freud's theory? Where does it leave the question of femininity? We may question the simplicity of the oedipal formula in which being and having are divided by recalling how this division breaks down in Freud's taxonomy of love. We see that constituting difference in the complementary form leads to the position of the feminine as not-Y. Thus Rose (1982) sets forth the idea that woman is the empty set, that language produces the feminine as its negative term, its other, lacking any essence. But why is it the feminine, once again only the feminine, that is constituted as a negative? Why is it only the work on femininity that leads, as Rose (1985) maintains, to the "collapse of the category of sexuality *as content* altogether"?

After all, the reversal that takes maternal identification as a point of departure showed that we can just as easily conceive of masculinity as the negative of the maternal, the not-mother, likewise an "empty set." It would be more plausible to view the sexual difference symmetrically, with each position as the negation of the other, each negating the other's claim to represent any content other than "I am not you." But that would be a subject-subject logic, an intersubjective view. The logic here is that of the subject-object positions, one side has to lose out. And therefore sexuality must appear to have a content, a specific determination that can justify this asymmetry. As we know, that justification is the special function of the phallus to signify difference.

Rose explains why the symmetrical reversal that destabilizes both masculinity and femininity is not acceptable. Here we have to consider a further piece of the Lacanian logic, regarding how we become subjects able to function at the symbolic level; this refers to the crucial capacity to represent our mental experience in a way that takes us out of the enclosed imaginary into the world of other subjects. Rose tells us that the objections to Lacan (and this applies to

Freud implicitly as well) that simply reverse his argument by defining femininity through the preoedipal identification with the mother rather than through the phallus leave the female outside the symbolic. To define woman in relation to woman, to have a girl's active femininity derive from her mother, would cut out the father and his phallus altogether, throw the girl into dyadic fusion without end. Such feminist theories wind up defending a presymbolic, maternal order and thereby only serve to reaffirm the fact that symbolization and separation do require the phallus.

But is this true? Following the line of argument that proceeds from Chasseguet-Smirgel (1976) through Chodorow (1978) and appears in my work as well, the separation-individuation conflict can be understood as sufficient to catapult the girl into seeking a relation to father, and indeed this impulse to separation moves her toward the symbolic in any case. I have also contended that the father in this context is used as a symbol of the intersubjective space initially created by the mother. The original dialogue with an outside other is the basis for the internal process of thinking and representing. The mother's dialogic ability stimulates the child's recognition of her subjectivity; as she represents and reflects back the child's own subjectivity, she initiates symbolic capacities. Failing this maternal activity of thinking, the father and penis do not become symbolic but are imagined as concrete "things" that make for difference. Thus to begin with the mother rather than the phallus is not necessarily to wind up defending a presymbolic maternal order nor to affirm by default that symbolization and separation do require the phallus (Benjamin, 1995c).

In any case, the mother of whom Rose speaks would not be a feminine mother—a mother who is castrated, who needs the phallus or father to complete her—but only a phallic mother. The crucial assumption here is that the mother must be split: Her femininity must be constituted through the negation of the phallic mother. As Chasseguet-Smirgel (1976) explains, the idea of the castrated woman functions as the negation of the child's unconscious maternal imago, of the preoedipal omnipotence attributed to her when the child was helplessly dependent upon her.

The questionable premise of this position is not the idea that the mother must desire another, that the child must realize she/he is not *mother's desire* (see Kristeva, 1986). It is that only by seeing her as castrated can the mother be seen as "not-all" (see Benjamin, 1995c). This castration refers her desire back to its origin in the oedipal girl who has nothing of her own (no organ, no desire), and so must turn to the father to gain a baby/penis. But the "castrated" mother cannot desire someone else—only by having her own organ can she do this. In an endless cycle, daughter turns away from mother, even as an object of identification, then becomes a mother whose desire can only be represented as have-not, passive, beloved of the man. Let us note once again the asymmetry of the sexes: Whereas the boy can have someone *like* mother, eventually, and as Freud insisted in *The Ego and the Id*, he may also be *like* the father ("You may be like me"); the girl turns away from mother, she does not move to a new level of identification with the oedipal mother. She does not move from trying to *be* the mother to being *like* the mother. Her love of the father must be mediated only by the phallus, not an identification with an active femininity represented by her mother's love of father as well as her. No triangular relation to mother after all, only a dyad to which she cannot return without sacrificing her symbolic subjectivity. Thus Freud, and Mitchell following him, has her "terminate her attachment" to mother and move to a new dyad with the father that repeats the old one.

In ordinary observation, to which Freud often appeals, we see that girls do not terminate their attachment to mother and they do retain an identification with her. The theory of Chodorow and other object relations thinkers (Fast, 1984; Ogden, 1987) has the advantage of recognizing that even when girls take their fathers as love objects they do not need, as Freud thought, to repudiate their love of the mother. On the contrary, such abrupt disillusionment would constitute a splitting of the object that would make love of an external, whole object unlikely (Ogden, 1987), giving father-love a wholly defensive character, that of "beating back the mother" (as in Chasseguet-Smirgel, 1976). It is far more likely that the girl, parallel to the boy, would produce an oedipal relation that includes an ambivalent stance of seeing her mother as rival and as loved figure of identification (as Horney or Klein would see it). She can, as Fast (1984) points out, develop her identification with the mother beyond a fused sense of being her to a more differentiated sense of being like her and other women in various ways.

Why would it be necessary to emphasize the girl's object love for the father to the exclusion of her identification with mother, and to make her femininity, or the riddle of sexual difference, depend upon it? Rather than allowing a mutual questioning of both femininity and masculinity that culminates in an acceptance of gender indeterminacy or a questioning of heterosexuality, the Lacanian position returns us to a reification of heterosexuality based upon a specific gender content.

Rather than ask how either child might move from the primary identification with mother to a sense of loving someone different from
themselves (see Chodorow, 1994) this position seems to return us only
to the impossibility of femininity. And yet, I think there is something
to this story. Chodorow's picture of the girl's femininity arising out of
the continuity with the preoedipal mother, set up against the opposing position of masculine separation and boundaries from mother,
needs to be augmented to encompass the sexual content of both positions, especially Freud's duality of activity/passivity. Freud's insistence that the feminine position is not identical with the maternal, that
femininity is constituted by a particular relation to the father and
phallus, reflected an important though incomplete insight—it too has
a truth, though this truth is not the whole story. It is only the powerful
story of patriarchy. It represents male dominance as more seamless
than it is, as if a complete dominance of the oedipal subject-object
complementary were the whole story, as if there were nothing behind
this story. Were there no other truth, this logic could never be deconstructed. It would not be possible for so much of our lived reality to
contradict the logic of this complementarity, and gender would not
appear so paradoxical, so incompletely realized, so constituted by
negation, one "empty set" facing another "empty set."

I am going to propose that there is something "behind" this
story, which is indeed exposed by our reversal in favor of a theory
that begins with the mother—a process behind the real appearances
of masculinity and femininity. This process of gendering is indeed
more complicated than the simple identification with the parent of
the same sex, which rests on an infinite reduction backward. In fact,
the clue to it is Freud's insistence that femininity comes into being
after and in contrast to the identification with the active mother. If
femininity is not constituted by a maternal identification—since that
identification occurs prior to the recognition of sexual difference—
we can wonder, nevertheless, why femininity and maternal identification are opposed, split apart.

I will suggest an explanation for this peculiar opposition between the maternal and the feminine, one which also sheds light on
the continual reoccurrence of the equation of femininity with passivity. As I discussed in the previous chapter, we might see the notion
of the feminine passive daughter somewhat as Horney (1926) saw
Freud's theory of female castration: a reflection of the mind of the
oedipal boy. In other words, Freud's theory reenacts the move in
which the oedipal boy, in order to claim activity for himself, repudi-

ates the baby/passive/incorporative position by putting the female into it. This then, contrary as it is to real maternal activity, becomes the so-called feminine position. Let us recall that for Freud (1914) the beloved, feminine object is after all created by the man's reversal, in which he makes her into the narcissistic object of adoration that he was as a baby. And he, even more unwittingly, plays the maternal part.

We are considering here the oedipal mother, who not only nurtures but evokes in the child excitement that cannot be satisfied and often not well-contained, which may be humiliating, frightening, or overstimulating. In short, if experienced passively, this stimulation might evoke the feeling of being her helpless object. In an early paper on the "Neuropsychosis of Defense" Freud (1896) makes clear his thinking that the obsessional position of defensive activity is the masculine way of repressing what would otherwise be experienced as the feminine passivity of overstimulation (Christiansen, 1993). Originally the mother's containing function actually ought to protect the child from helpless overstimulation. Her ability to represent the child's state of mind and draw him into the safer symbolic world should help make his feelings tolerable and allow him to see her as a subject rather than a dangerous object. But if the boy is barred from incorporating that function through identification, or if he is too flooded to develop ownership of desire, what does he do? He must adopt a defensive activity. Unable to be his own container, he must instead defensively use the activity of discharge into the object who contains. In this sense, the masculine defense entails neither separation nor boundaries but an urgently driven relation to the object. This is activity without authorship or ownership—hence, without the genuine subjectivity that allows space for another subject.

This driven activity is the counterpart to feminine passivity. As Brennan (1992) has elaborated in a parallel argument, the masculine form of active mastery demands a feminine object to take up the feelings of helpless passivity one is trying to get rid of.[5] To take up these feelings now includes being a container for male dis-

---

[5] Brennan (1992) develops an idea of energy exchange in which the subject gains energy by fixing the other in the "feminine" position. The daughter, or occupant of that position receives the father's "imprint," the unwanted anxiety, being used to provide the "living attention" that sustains the self. While this fixing of identity suppresses multiplicity, in Brennan's view either sex can assume the masculine position.

charge, for the evacuated feelings—an object without a desire of her own. This object of demand is translated as the oedipal daughter who switches to passivity, renounces activity, and becomes the vessel for the paternal penis/baby. In other words, a more passive, controllable container than the mother was—though also because of this a potentially stimulating one, and in cases of incest, one in whom to literally discharge.

We can now see how femininity becomes the negative of maternal activity or, perhaps, a perversion of mothering. In Chasseguet-Smirgel's (1976) exposition, this construction of femininity is shared by male and female oedipal children in reaction to the sense of helplessness before the mother's enormous power. The castrated "feminine" position is precisely the negative of the omnipotent position of the maternal imago in the unconscious. As I see it, the maternal object is split: femininity as absorbtion, accommodation and receptivity, is constituted as the antidote opposing the phallic mother's control. Indeed, this split off femininity, the cancellation of maternal power, may be used to oppose the relational capacities that Chodorow sees as evolving in the preoedipal relation to mother; it may emphasize the baby rather than the mother aspect of the dyad. For now the feminine position becomes the position the daughter takes up in order to separate from mother and displace her power onto the father. Whether she does this in direct compliance to him or in her aspiration to the cultural representation of femininity, she may now renounce the identification with the father and recast what she has imbibed as maternal holding into passive receptivity. At the clinical level, we may note that the girl may already have had to function as mother's container, her accommodating object, and may now use the father to escape that position, to free her sexuality from a more confining "unfreedom." (Dinnerstein, 1976). At the cultural level, we might say that this sexual form of femininity—object of male desire—meets the girl at the moment she needs to separate and offers her a route into the world of men. While the cultural form of femininity serves both girl's and boy's revolt against the maternal, it still may be seen, broadly speaking, as the effect of a male construction of culture in accord with the oedipal boy's anxieties.

Reading the Lacanian account, we can say that there, too, the feminine is first constituted by the oedipal boy's act of dividing the mother. When the boy entering the symbolic breaks his identification with her, it is precisely the *feminine* mother with whom he disidentifies; meanwhile on the level of the imaginary she remains phallic, not feminine but masculine, and he keeps his identification with her, as the sexually controlling, regulating, active partner. The feminine is first constituted by this act of dividing the mother. From this perspective, by definition, the girl can only be feminine by identifying with the part of the mother not kept by the boy. Yet, she can only separate from mother by becoming feminine in this sense; by being the daughter, rather than, say, the mother's mother (another favorite position for the daughter).

Femininity in this sense is the negative of the masculine but also does have a determinate content: It is defined by the boy's oedipal repudiation of the maternal and relocation of the mother-baby dyad in the daughter. Thus the oedipal turn to the father, by which the girl distinguishes herself from maternal identification in accord with her father's oedipal wishes, is the "true" feminine. This is a gender truth that, although "false," makes sense of Freud's opposition between maternal activity and feminine passivity, and of the equation, sexual difference equals the girl's heterosexual orientation. But something else underwrites this truth. The constitution of this form of sexual difference also rests upon the fear of passivity and helplessness (Chasseguet-Smirgel, 1976). The "content" of femininity is to contain this unwanted, primitively feared experience and make of it an exciting invitation, something that the phallus can now act upon, control, and structure. In this sense, femininity, unlike motherhood (which is so ambiguously active and powerful), is the position of the object in relation to the subject. What I have tried to show is that this construction of femininity—and its counterpart, masculinity as resistance to passivity—is not the inevitable form taken by sexual difference but a psychic construction of the male oedipal position, which has stamped the gender divide with its meaning.

Oedipal Complementarity and Preoedipal Inclusivity, or, the Phenomenology of Identification and Object Love

I have shown how the oedipal construction of masculinity and femininity in Freud's version of the Oedipus complex exemplified the subject-object complimentarity. The principle of mutual exclusivity, with or without determinations, the principle that one can be X and have Y or be Y and have X, seems to be the underlying ordering principle. It is the principle of the oedipal position, of heterosexuality, and it is everywhere in evidence. Yet this principle is not seamless; it is continually overturned by multiplicity and gender ambiguity, producing the paradox we noted earlier. Many individuals who have formed a sexual subjectivity do not, as Freud himself pointed out, conform to this principle: One can be masculine and love a man, be feminine and love a woman. Identification and object choice do not always remain in inverse relation.

Indeed, as our reading of "On Narcissism" showed, idealization in object love seems to represent a very particular kind of transmutation of identification. The distinction between object love and identification may be as elusive as that between femininity and masculinity, the difference that engenders sexual love as elusive as the content of sexual difference. Object love may be as much a riddle as femininity. As we pursue our phenomenology of gender complementarity we shall consider how the split between identification and object love works in the oedipal formation, and perhaps shed some light on these riddles as well.

To anticipate, I will suggest how a view of the postoedipal that integrates preoedipal currents, overcoming the antithetical relation of preoedipal and oedipal, offers a different form of complementarity, which disrupts the logic of mutual exclusivity. While it does not abolish the logic of X equals not-Y, Y equals not-X, it recognizes that these identities, Y and X, can be recombined in more complicated equations $(A = 5x + 2y-x)$, thereby producing gender multiplicity. Femininity and masculinity, which create each other as "not-you," are recombined in ways that further question their content and stability. This produces the paradox already noted above, that people can be heterosexual or homosexual, love Y and be Y, love X and be X—a paradox that ultimately makes one ask, Why is it that a man who loves a woman and acts "feminine" is considered heterosexual but a man who loves another man and acts as his opposite is not? If an intersubjective perspective opens up a way of transcending the subject-object relationship, and hence of a different relationship of activity and passivity, it may point a way toward overcoming that logic of exclusive, polarized identities. I (Benjamin, 1991; 1995b), along with others (especially Aron 1995; Bassin, 1997), have proposed that this overcoming is rooted in the recuperation of preoedipal overinclusiveness that does not abolish the oedipal division, but often transcends or suspends it.

Let me begin by reviewing some of the object relational thinking about gender differentiation that informed the last decades. As I discussed earlier, Stoller's work offered a reversal of Freud's position, setting out the idea that all children begin with a primary identification with mother. However, alongside that identification, Stoller postulated an early recognition of one's own assignation to male or female, which he called core gender identity (Stoller, 1968). This notion of a kinesthetic sensibility, a sense of body ego based on the way one is treated by others, is one that might be better conceived as *nominal* gender identity—a child becomes organized by it as it does by a name. One difficulty with the concept is that at the time of its inception, there was as yet no theory of preverbal, presymbolic representation, such as Stern (1985) and Beebe (Beebe & Lachmann, 1994) have now proposed. Stoller (1973) had to speculate that the earliest sense of gender might be transmitted through something prerepresentational, like contagion. Current theorizing makes it possible to anchor a notion of early identification in representations, making early identifications more comparable to later ones, albeit based in more concrete sensory-motor schemas.

Another difficulty in the original formulation of the core gender identity concept arose from the fact that Stoller developed it without filling in the period between its culmination and the oedipal, skipping the preoedipal as it were. The preoedipal period, to the degree that it was elucidated, seemed to be occupied primarily by the process of disidentification from mother, an idea which Greenson (1968) introduced. Thus the model looked something like this (at least for the boy): Establish core gender identity, disidentify from mother, enter the oedipal. Obviously, our thinking about the preoedipal has greatly expanded since that formulation. Person and Ovesey (1983) added to this model, filling its lacuna by suggesting that during the separation-individuation period children of both sexes must disidentify from mother and consolidate gender role identity. This view saw girls and boys as more symmetrical in their separation process, but explained that boy's separation difficulties would tend to leave a more visible marker.

My suggestion (Benjamin, 1995b), based on Fast's (1984; 1990) formulations about overinclusive, bisexual identifications as well as my own observations, is that neither boys nor girls disidentify from the primary parent at this time. They do become more separate and they do try to use a second figure—stereotypically the less primary, more coming and going parent, but often another available, attached adult or older sibling—to support individuation. In a traditional family, therefore, children of both sexes will, during rapprochement, differentiate mother and father as source of goodness and subject of desire respectively. As Abelin (1980) pointed out, the toddler moves from the concreteness of the sensory-motor cognition, in which she experiences the attraction as emanating from the object, to a subjective, symbolic mode—she knows that *she* wants *it*. She can represent this capacity to be a subject of desire symbolically, by seeing someone else express this kind of intentionality and authorship. I (Benjamin, 1986a, b; 1988; 1991; 1995b) differed from Abelin in thinking that the primary object of desire is less likely to be Mommy—although in his example the birth of a new sibling made that plausible—than to be the outside world, with which the child had begun the practicing love affair (Mahler, Pine & Bergmann, 1975). In practicing, the world has come to be experienced as an extension of that first exciting, loved other. In rapprochement, the child has a love affair with the father who represents that exciting, compelling outside world; he is the figure of freedom who has access to and enjoys the world.

The sense of being a subject of desire, and hence a primary sense of subjectivity, is thus informed not merely by lack, or entry into the oedipal symbolic, but by a prior symbolizing relation (but not fully symbolic—imaginary, if you will) to the father or comparable figure who represents the kind of authorship and intentionality the child is first formulating. Identificatory love is a specific formation, it is the love that wants to be recognized by the other as like. Identification is not merely a matter of incorporating the ideal, but of loving and having a relationship with the person who embodies the ideal (such as Freud, 1914b, described). This love is actually directed more outside than the original love of the source of goodness, a fact Freud (1921) might have had in mind when he called the identificatory tie the first tie to the object and associated it with the father. It is a step toward recognizing the other as subject, although its aim is to incorporate that other rather than fully accept the otherness. I suggested that identificatory love in this form is homoerotic, whether it is the boy's or girl's toward the father; it is used both to ratify sameness and bridge difference.

In linking identificatory love to the rapprochement father, I was emphasizing that the father figure is used not merely to beat back the mother, to defensively idealize someone other than mother, but also to extend love to a second (Domenici, personal communication). I emphasized that the father, or any other second person, can be just as effective for the daughter as for the son in supporting the child's sense of being a subject of desire. I also emphasized that the boy does not need to forgo identification with mother so early, unless difficulties in separation lead to an early defensive repudiation. This defensive constellation highlights the magical, omnipotent aspects of the paternal figure rather than his figuring of agency and authorship. It also leads to a premature oedipal splitting between the powerful father and engulfing mother.

In this view, identificatory love of the father might also explain the phenomenon that Freud thought so difficult to understand, the girl's turn to the father. But it suggests that this turn occurs earlier, as an addition to rather than a supplanting of the relation to the mother, as a move to incorporate activity rather than renounce it. To be sure, this turn does not explain what makes fathers different from mothers, but is based upon an existing difference, a social postulate of the father who stands in a different relation to the world, the culture, the "outside." That is why, increasingly, it appears unlinked to anatomy, and more like a social role that can be adopted by parents of either sex. Yet, despite this detachment from the anatomical, we are well aware that it is precisely such historically long-established positions that inform our phenomenology of gender, our sense of the masculine and feminine. The unconscious mapping of these positions continues to saturate our affective experience of excitement and anxiety about difference. The conjunction of identification and pregenital erotic excitement in an idealizing love of a powerful figure already contains many aspects of what will later figure as romantic love. Thus it may be that, as Freud's (1914b) suggestions in "On Narcissism" imply, the idealization of the love object is always a transposition of this identificatory love, and in that sense object love and identificatory love are two sides of the same coin.

The original constellation in which erotic love and identification meet is, however, far more fluid than the metaphor of two sides suggests. Before the oedipal principle of mutual exclusivity is instituted, a phase of gender differentiation exists that Fast (1984) has termed overinclusive. In this period preoedipal children try to encompass sexual difference by incorporating what they learn about the other's body inside themselves, forming bisexual identifications and elaborating them. In their bodily play and representations, children make analogies to cross-sex experience. They imagine they can be and have everything, and create representations of both sexes through this fantasy. At first, the contradiction of being and not being X or Y is only a vague shadow. Increasingly, the cross-sex identifications are highlighted in protest as they begin to learn about anatomy as a binary system of sexual difference. Recognizing the scheme of bodily difference, they nonetheless imagine themselves as able to hold the opposites inside. Thus, boys express envy of female reproductive capacities and organs, girls of male organs, not yet acceding to the principle of mutual exclusivity.[6] Castration at this point means, for both sexes, the loss of that which links you to the object through identification, having the same thing she or he has.

The question that has been raised (May, 1986) is whether, as Fast contends, children actually have to renounce this preoedipal overinclusiveness and establish a firm and definite gender identity, or whether we can conceptualize the matter somewhat differently. May (1986), Aron (1995), and Bassin (1997) have objected to Fast's use of the term *renunciation* to describe the child's giving up of aspiration to bisexual completeness and the capacities of the opposite sex.

I believe I did not recognize a certain contradiction in *The Bonds of Love*. I agreed with Fast that the child renounces certain opposite-sex identifications and allows them to be the prerogative of the other, thus transforming homoerotic identification into a basis for heteroeroticism; but I also claimed that cross-sex identifications persist and "can subsequently become the basis for later flexibility, so that in the individual's mind the gendered self-representation coexists with a genderless or even opposite-gendered self-representation." This harkens back to Freud's observation of the heterosexual man with feminine behavior, the homosexual who acts masculine. While it might be true that object choice often emerges as a transmutation of relinquished identification, this is not the whole story. This contradiction could be solved by further differentiating between sexual and nonsexual representations, as if only sexual identifications with the other are relinquished—but that assumes a narrow and oversimplified picture of sexuality, contrary to the whole spirit of psychoanalysis. It might be more useful to postulate that this contradiction reflects an important aspect of psychic reality: the tension between the dominance of the oedipal principle and the persistence of preoedipal overinclusiveness.

---

[6] Fast stresses a certain asymmetry, that boys mainly envy reproductive capacities, but I have been struck by clinical and childhood evidence that some males also have fantasies of having a vagina or uterus; in response to lectures on this subject I have been told of men whose unwanted sexual compulsions dissolved as they recovered the fantasy of having a vagina.

In other words, the oedipal does not simply abolish the over-inclusivity that precedes it. Aron (1995) has suggested that we think not of phases that supercede one another, but positions that coexist. Rather than postulating that the overinclusive phase be fully super-ceded by the oedipal phase, it might oscillate with it, Aron says, as the depressive and paranoid-schizoid positions oscillate. Thus we could say that, in one position, we attribute certain elements to the other, in another position, we consider them to be free-floating attributes of self and other. While these positions develop phase-specifically, they become coexistent. Nor is there evidence that overinclusive aspirations are inherently a sign of psychosis, as the Lacanian link between sexual division and subjectivity supposes. Rather, many individuals can tolerate highly different self-repre-sentations, if continuity of nominal gender identification and repre-sentation of the oedipal position are maintained. Even high degrees of ambiguity are not the same as dedifferentiation or psychosis—for nominal gender identification provides a frame for conflicting and discordant lines.

The capacity to tolerate conflict, and indeed the capacity to split the ego and take up antithetical positions, may, in certain con-ditions, be potentially creative as well as a more common feature of sexual enjoyment than is usually supposed. I am tempted to think that a benign form of splitting the ego in relation to gender may well be an important accomplishment: "I know I'm not That, but I feel like That." It allows us to own our conflicting aspirations and yet ac-cept our limits. Identification with otherness necessarily throws us into paradox: I both am and am not the thing with which I identify (see Dimen, 1991). I have to be able to accept the impossibility of in-corporating otherness, but retain the ability to imagine it without being threatened or undone by it. Identification must be tolerated in order that the other's qualities not evoke intolerable envy or fear. Since we recognize that all sexual fantasies and all identifications (conscious and unconscious) must achieve a level of symbolism dis-tinct from the concreteness of anatomy, then anatomically correct identification is not necessarily a sign of psychic differentiation. Sex-uality demands a metaphorical rather than a concrete understand-ing of the body.

To return to the idea of two oscillating stances in regard to our gender. It can be argued that without access to the overinclusive identifications, the oedipal renunciation inevitably elides into repu-diation, splitting the difference, rather than truly recognizing it (Ben-

64

jamin, 1995b). In fact, differentiation in the oedipal phase is not the final achievement that has often been supposed by psychoanalytic theory. It is based on a principle of mutual exclusivity that is not fully realistic and does not, initially, square with an appreciative recognition of difference. This should not be surprising, inasmuch as oedipal castration anxiety makes difference clearer than in the pre-oedipal but also more threatening. Castration means different things in different phases. Whereas in the preoedipal situation the narcissistic blow comes with the admission that one cannot have what the other has, in the oedipal phase, one fears that if one persists in wanting what the other has, one will lose one's own organs, identity, and gendered body (Fast, 1984).

Mayer (1985) has suggested that the fear of losing one's own genitals is as crucial for oedipal girls as it is for boys, and accompanied by same-sex chauvinism, insistence that "everyone must be just like me," repudiation of the other. Interestingly, Mayer's case illustrates the oedipal anxiety around mutual exclusivity and how it must be transcended as a condition for heterosexual love. A patient dreamed that she grew a penis, and dropped a basket of eggs that smashed. The dream seemed to reflect an identification with a man the patient was dating, an identification she had always strenuously rejected. Acknowledging the threat to her feminine identity posed by this masculine identification allowed her to subsequently feel closer to him and tolerate his (previously intolerable and frightening) difference from her.

This is the typical challenge posed by the oedipal position: How is the threatening distance of not being the same to be negotiated? By having the other rather than being the same. But initially, the oedipal child cannot yet have either. Thus, of necessity, the first oedipal round ends in incomplete acceptance of difference, neither having nor being the other. The ensuing resentment based on unresolved envy of the other is especially apparent in latency children in our culture. The incomplete mourning expresses itself in aggression and chauvinism.

Another aspect of the oedipal anxiety, in this case the negative oedipal, underlies homophobia: fear that if one persists in desiring the object that the other is supposed to desire one might lose one's own gender identity (Stoller, 1973). Of course, this belief—the underpinning of anxiety about homosexuality (Butler, 1990)—is no less magical thinking than the preoedipal, based on a primitive sense of identification: If I want the same thing she wants, I will become her.

In fact, we should note that it is difficult to distinguish here between these two thoughts: If I continue to want to have the capacities a girl (mother) has, I will lose what I have and turn into a girl (mother); if I long for father like a girl (mother) does, I will turn into a girl. By linking these two thoughts, the oedipal position establishes the heterosexual system under the aegis of the idea of mutual exclusivity.

To generalize, complementarity becomes an organizing principle in the oedipal phase, and gender complementarity is internalized as an ideal (Goldner, 1991), however adverse to the complex reality of an individual's desires and identifications. One cannot yet embody the ideal of femininity or masculinity that mother and father purportedly represent, and one cannot yet "possess" the other body in love; one cannot be or have. The cultural ideal of masculinity impedes mourning or sublimating the identification with the mother; it thus splits the mother and demands, as we have seen, a derogated feminine as its negative counterpart. In other words, identification inverted as object love under the aegis of mutual exclusivity leads to the dual problems Freud noted regarding femininity and masculinity: The girl must take up a passive position renouncing the desiring subjectivity attained through identification with the father; the boy must defend himself against femininity and his identification with mother by taking a contemptuous stance toward the female sex. Activity and passivity become opposing terms, culminating in a mass of contradictions.

Fortunately, however, the opposition between object love and identificatory love is only clear cut and organizing for the sexual experience of the oedipal position (see Loewald, 1976), which is not the end- or be-all of sexuality. The oedipal organization is, however, the dominant one and is deeply allied with the gender bifurcation in the structure of heterosexuality. This structure gives rise to a crucial paradox, as the feminist critic, Jane Gallop (1988), has pointed out: Since the phallic masculinity theorized by Freud is organized around have and have not, it is precisely not "a masculine that can couple with a feminine." Indeed, Breen (1996) shows how the phallus as ideal of self-completion suppresses the penis as an organ of bodily desire rather than linking penis and vagina. Thus, the oedipal complementarity spawns the contradiction between its loving aim and its gender form. It is indeed worth asking whether the alignment of activity with the masculine subject and femininity with the passive object, while undoubtedly inscribed in erotic life, is the only basis for the heteroerotic.

At the very least, we can say that the oedipal opposition between object love and identification is not the only possible relationship between being like and loving. Likewise, identificatory and object love may not be as distinct or opposed as has often been assumed. From this it follows that the distinction between heterosexuality and homosexuality is—at the level of psychic experience, as opposed to the social level that relies on nominal gender—far more ambiguous. For being a like subject or a love object are often complementing, interwoven, aspects of a relationship (Harris, 1991). Nor is it possible to assume that heterosexual love is necessarily based on complementarity. As we have seen, a girl's identificatory love may become the basis for her object choice, as Freud had noted in his remarks on narcissism. I have discussed elsewhere (Benjamin, 1986a; 1991) the way in which frustrated identificatory love spurs woman's ideal love of the man she might have wished to be, often taking the form of a masochistic self-debasement. But this can be no less true for a man, whose female love object may represent aspects of the unattainable father ideal.

The assumption that identification necessarily opposes object love makes real homoeroticism unthinkable (O'Connor & Ryan, 1993). Butler (1990) points out that the psychoanalytic concept of bisexuality still excludes homosexuality insofar as it merely allows each person to take up both heterosexual positions, but never proposes that like can love like. Her strategy is to propose a reversal based on Freud. In effect she argues that the normally understood identification with the same-sex parent might well be understood as the "precipate of abandoned object cathexes" (Freud, 1917), the melancholic residue of tabooed homosexual love (Butler, 1995). In other words, homosexual love would precede bisexual identification, rather than being an expression of it. This proposition would be valid if all identification sprang from abandoned love. However, it may not be necessary to suppose that identification is derivative of object love; rather we can theorize the primacy of the identificatory tie alongside object love. In that case, identification would not be merely a melancholic response to loss; neither, however, would object love be merely a solution to lost identification.

Thus, we need not set up an inverse relationship between identification and object love where one must "cause" or precede into the other. We could speculate that in original identificatory love, such as that for the rapprochement father, the two positions are not yet split: Love of the different and striving for sameness do not yet appear contradictory. If the antithesis between object love and identification only constitutes one possible structure, the oedipal, then heterosexuality and homosexuality also appear less polarized. Each erotic position can be seen as involving particular combinations of identification and object love.

It now becomes possible to disentangle the pathologizing equation that psychoanalytic theory has made between opposite-sex identification, homosexuality, and denial of the primal scene. Aron (1995) has suggested a reconsideration of the Kleinian view of the primal scene, which can be reconceptualized as a field of multiple identifications. The hallmark of achieving a more differentiated position in relation to the primal scene would not be the acceptance of heterosexual, genital complementarity but the achievement of intersubjective triangularity. The primal scene confronts the child with the difficulty of having to decide with whom to identify, whom to be, and whom to have. In the oedipal phase, this may well require taking up the position, If I *am* X, I *love* Y and conversely, if I *love* Y, I *am* X. Or if I *am* Y, I *love* X, and conversely if I *love* Y, I *am* X. But from an intersubjective perspective, the importance of the triangular scene is that the child represents itself as subject and object, participant and observer, outside the relationship between two others (whole objects). Aron's logic is that the important thing is for each parent to be differentiated, and thus for the child to be able to recognize the separateness of each point on the triangle. The intersubjective capacity at stake here is that of both participating and observing in the same relationship. This is crucial to the analytic endeavor, allowing a splitting of the ego which tolerates different perspectives on our positions (Aron & Harris, 1993), expanding what we can own.

What is decisive for propelling the child into oedipal differentiation is the realization that X and Y have a relationship outside oneself, a relationship that one can only enter through identification with one of them. However, the key point is to be able to imagine the partner as separate or different. Thus, whether one identifies with X or Y, same or opposite sex, is not decisive for differentiation. To identify with X (opposite) rather than Y (same) is neither inherently dedifferentiating of one's parents nor denying of nominal gender identification. While it may be true that sexuality organized by compulsive, perverse scenarios represents an attack or denial of the genital primal scene, it does not follow conversely that allegiance to the genital complementarity is free of such attacks or denials, that such allegiance is a necessary or sufficient condition for differentiated sexuality. The adherence to a rigid oedipal formulation of genital heterosexuality may only serve to stabilize the dissociation of other elements of identification and desire, elements then perceived as an attack endangering the self.

Even as we have seen that this principle of mutual exclusivity does not operate in a compelling way for many individuals, we have also seen that each psyche is capable of holding multiple positions—those who like Y and act like Y, for instance, may be operating on the basis of more subtle differentiations (Y1, Y2, Y6–2) than those who accept the simple antithesis (X ≠ Y). We may conclude that the link between object choice and gender identification, which Freud first formulated in relation to the Oedipus complex, is one among many in the chain of gender positions. The complex amalgam of gender—often composed of several contradictory positions—that an individual takes to be her or his "identity" involves not merely an identification that is the obverse of object choice. Homosexual choice is not simply the "inversion" of the heterosexual pattern; for instance, it is not necessarily more infused with identificatory love than heterosexuality. How might we, then, think about the ongoing relationship between object love and identification, and the fate of identificatory love later in life? How might the integration of the earlier over-inclusive position after the establishment of oedipal complementarity contribute to a higher level of differentiation, which can tolerate the lived ambiguities of gender? The two questions are related.

Transcending Oedipal Complementarity

My proposal, based on the foregoing, is that the sustaining of identificatory tendencies alongside object love creates a different kind of complementarity, and a different stance towards oppositional differences. As I have stated before (Benjamin, 1995b) it is necessary to distinguish between two forms of complementarity. The earlier, oedipal form is a simple opposition, constituted by splitting, projecting the unwanted elements into the other; unconsciously, the other's position is known but is represented as not-self, threatening to one's sense of identity. The position of the other may be idealized or depreciated, or seen as a mirror of what the self has, in other words, its receptacle. The postoedipal complementarity reintegrates elements of identification, so that they become less threatening, less diametrically

69

opposite, no longer cancelling out one's identity. This position is vital in sustaining erotic relations with someone perceived as other. For the sense of difference to be exciting and pleasurable rather than merely threatening, the self must be able to bear an attunement with the other that revives earlier feelings of identification.

Before going further, I should make some brief comments on my usage of the postoedipal as a developmental term. In general, from a clinical point of view, one need only think of positions, not phases. But I think that these positions do originally occur sequentially: for instance, the postoedipal reflects a transcendence of an already organized oedipal polarity, and that requires that it come about later, as we do observe. But critics fear that any postulate of developmental sequence gives rise to the problem of normativity (Lesser, 1997). Coates (1997) has made an effort to reconcile the poststructural critique of normativity and the use of developmental research and thought. She proposes a jettisoning of "developmental lines," which means the necessary coincidence and coherence of accomplishments across domains, without giving up the idea of sequence ("a child cannot learn to run before he or she knows how to stand up. A child does not develop gender constancy until he or she is capable of making gender discriminations.") In this sense, different positions make different contributions, and these do not necessarily occur simultaneously. In effect, this is an argument for separating different development accomplishments and recognizing that they do not all fit together neatly. So, by suggesting that the intersubjective aspect of visualizing the parents' separate relationship ("oedpial exclusion") is not to be equated with a particular form of heterosexual identification, I am separating the development of self-other representation, gender and sexual object choice. Coates' more complex view of development does raise an important question regarding the oedipal joining of the principle of mutual exclusivity with heterosexual complementarity: why do these appear to go hand in hand?

While it is surely observable that in our culture most children must traverse and absorb the stance of oedipal complementarity—insisting on polarity, mutual exclusivity, black and white, male and female, have and have not—this observation has misled many into considering the oedipal complementarity an endpoint of development making, the postoedipal a mere footnote. By the same token, any divergence from the oedipal is seen as a regression. I have proposed that we compare the stance toward gender with Kohlberg's (1981) moral development theory, with its distinction between conventional and postconventional thinking. We could say that this oedipal polarizing corresponds to conventional thinking about difference, which is appropriate to this stage of children's moral and cognitive development. In Kohlberg's view, postconventional thinking can begin to develop in adolescence, with the capacity to read the spirit rather than the letter of the law, and to make one's own judgments.

This distinction has a counterpart in the Lacanian distinction between the "small" other who merely represents the law and "God," the unmanifest, "big" Other who is taken to be the Law: Conflating the two represents a collapse of the symbolic (Zizek, 1995). Maintaining the differentiation between the ideal and its representative, these distinctions require the transcendence of the symbolic equation (Segal, 1957), in which a thing *is* what it represents. In this sense, the capacity for true symbolic thinking is accompanied by a more flexible, less absolute relationship to the principle of complementarity.

Working from a similar perspective, Bassin (1997) has argued that the transcendence of polarity in gender relations is expressed in symbol formation. She proposes a redeployment of the terms of genital theory, according to which the phallic phase, with its opposites have/have not, should give way in adolescence to a true genital phase, in which antithetical elements can be reunited. Unlike projective identification, symbolization reunites the antagonistic tendencies (Freedman, 1980; 1985), for instance active and passive, phallic and containing. Postoedipal symbolization links rather than prohibits the gratification of both aims (Bassin, 1997), expressing rather than masking the unconscious oscillation between them. The key to this symbolic function is the recuperation of identification with the "missing half" of the complementarity.

Samuels (1985) offers a Jungian view of symbols similar to this one, in which symbols serve to reconcile opposites and in so doing give expression to a sense of awe and power. He cites a woman patient who dreamed of a pitchfork, which had both feminine curves and phallic points, horrific nipples nonetheless connected to fertility. In line with this idea, an analyst reported to me a woman's dream in which a tampon seemed to represent something powerful, both phallic and a container for blood, which was both fertile and messy. We should also note that opposites need not always be reconciled, but can be accepted without splitting. Thus certain symbols reflect ambiguity about the meaning of the "thing," or, make it a transitional one: We cannot say whether it is masculine or feminine.

71

The postoedipal recuperation of overinclusivity also makes it possible to express different sexual positions in the same narrative without threat to the psyche. That is, it allows for a kind of multiplicity regarding gender (Dimen, 1995) that has recently been espoused by analysts who see each person as containing a multiplicity of selves (Bromberg, 1993, 1996; S. Mitchell, 1993; Davies, 1996; Pizer, 1996; Slavin, 1996). One is able to be aware of different positions, such that the evocation of one does not imply a threat to the other. In my essay on the father-daughter relationship (Benjamin, 1991), I described a patient who clearly sought in the transference the identificatory bond with the father as subject of desire. This woman was well able to work in the field of postoedipal complementarity. Identificatory and object love, oedipal and preoedipal themes converged in her symbols and narratives. In her struggle to separate from mother she enlisted both the imagery of the feminine and the identification with her brother and father.

To illustrate the postoedipal symbolic, let me refer to her dream of having to return the boots her brother gave her for Christmas. The boots had been very stylish, had been like a pair the analyst had, and fit very well. In the dream she has to return them for larger ones, that come up over the knee and don't fit well. She associates this with her mother returning the purse the brother had given her for Christmas, which was too small and kittenish, in other words, too feminine. The boots, both phallic objects and feminine containers, symbolize a full sexuality, that is, able to incorporate bi-gendered aspects of self. However, we note the split between the phallic mother and the feminine daughter here: The mother seems to oppose both the sexual and feminine aspects. She represents the demand for phallic control, which requires the patient to take boots that are engulfing, phallic in a sense that negates the sexual—the image of narcissistic self-sufficiency rather than the penis or the vagina that can couple with another. She states that her mother would let her have a penis, but not a "sexy" one (a symbol of her desire). By contrast, the patient's admired older brother represents a figure of identificatory love, one who helps her to separate from mother, as well as a person who recognizes her and knows what fits her. Subsequent associations about her brother made clear that he was a figure of ideal love, whose occasional rejection caused her deep humiliation. But he is most often associated with the analyst and other older women who had come to represent a subject of desire with whom to identify.

72

To further exemplify the interrelation of identificatory and object love: Some time later the patient, who associated her passionless husband with the restrictive controlling mother, went on to have a flirtation with her former college boy friend, a spirited, ardent, but unfaithful young man. She remembered that she had been at a college picnic, participating in a hoop race, wearing high heeled sandals, and the boyfriend had called to her from the sidelines, "Take off your shoes." She had kicked them off, and was able to run. Her comment was, she realized that what she was seeking with him was not actually a love partner. But his recognition was important because he, unlike her mother, had not needed her to win the race for him, he won his own races. Her heterosexual passion for this man thus included identificatory currents, which, once recognized, allowed her to realize what she was looking for in herself without feeling that she was dependent on him to separate from her husband.

The more differentiated postconventional relation to gender is one that includes, perhaps quite unselfconsciously, gender ambiguity and uncertainty. It allows a kind of symbolic thinking in which the complementarity opposite is no longer concrete and projected outward. The principle of division persists, but is also continually intertwined with the identificatory position that takes the other as like rather than merely opposite, as a supplement rather than a negation. As I have said before (Benjamin, 1995b), while the postconventional complementarity allows the multiplicity and mutuality denied by the oedipal form, it does not exist "outside" the terms of the gender division. It cannot, does not discover something wholly different, as yet unrepresented or unrepresentable. Rather, it remains in relation to that division, reworking its terms, disrupting its binary logic by recombining and breaking down opposites.

But this process of recombining makes a considerable difference. Even while it does not abolish the oedipal complementarity, it does subvert it, using the leverage of its own negative tension— the impossibility of constituting a complementary system that can truly exclude all identification with otherness from the self. The postconventional complementarity relies on the psychic capacity to symbolically bridge split oppositions as well as on preoedipal over-inclusiveness. It allows for transgression that recognizes rather than manically denies the necessity of separation and difference.

Such manic denial would, after all, only reaffirm the necessity of what it opposes. It has been stated before (Chodorow, 1985) that earlier radical theorists, like Brown and Marcuse, in advocating a pre-genital polymorphism tied to a period before the knowledge of difference, inadvertently validate the patriarchal logic. Their utopia always identifies the maternal with an undifferentiated world, before the law of the father enforces difference, thus, as Rose said, reaffirming the necessity of the paternal principle. Implicitly, individuation is enforced rather than desired. My argument differs from theirs insofar as I believe it is possible to recuperate the overinclusive without losing differentiation, still transcending the binary opposition in its oedipal form. Such a possibility exists precisely because differentiation is not necessarily opposed to but also infused with our desire. The self can, indeed must, hold multiple positions. Multiplicity may be seen as an effect of the attraction to difference as well as of the ongoing process of identification. If identification means the psychic tendency to continually incorporate or "eat up" everything we like, it is still an unavoidable part of our psychic condition. Releasing ourselves from the constraints of polarized oppositions means establishing identifications in a less absolute way, not fixed as the One or the Other—allowing entry into the transitional "third" place beyond identity.

The claim that the oedipal division institutes the renunciation of omnipotence, an acceptance of limits—being only the One or the Other, the only possible entry into the symbolic—now appears more problematic, a real appearance that is ultimately false. It fails to distinguish sufficiently between the concrete and the symbolic, thus continually reverting to reifications of sexual difference (that is, feminine equals passive). It misses the dimension of bridging difference through symbolic forms that depend upon identification. Such forms give depth to the delineation of difference, lifting it above the simple form of the oedipal complementarity, which has always concealed the unconscious narcissism and chauvinism of, "I am the one, you are the Other."

The reality of sexual differences is far more multifarious than the binary logic of mutual exclusivity allows. That logic, which ties us into thinking in terms of the opposition masculine/feminine, obscures a fundamental tension (or should we say, superordinate logic)—that between dimorphism and polymorphism, the logic of two and the logic of the many. In the logic of polymorphism we are not wedded to opposites, and difference is not constituted by simple complementarity.

Does this mean that the possibility exists (on some distant horizon where parallel lines meet) that sustaining a tension rather than splitting activity and passivity might abolish gender categories as we know them? I am inclined to think this unlikely because I see the tendency toward splitting as a fundamental piece of psychic reality, one which finds its expression in objective forms of culture and social life. The question is whether such splits in the self and in our theory have to be reified, congealed in massive cultural formations, perceived as the Law. In theory, it is possible to work through that process of reification, to elaborate what it conceals. In practice, we experience the loosening of those reifications in the free play of desire.

Conclusion

Let us return, then, for a final glance at the problem with which we began, the construction of gender along the opposition of activity and passivity. As we have seen in our analysis of Freud, the equation of "true" femininity with passivity played no small role in the construction of oedipal gender categories. It was, and continues to be, central to the theoretical defense of the principle of sexual difference identified with heterosexual complementarity. So let us undertake one last act of reversal, at least to begin deconstructing the terms of the polarity between activity and passivity.

Our earlier discussion of the boy's oedipal move showed how the male psyche constitutes femininity as the recipient of its defensive activity. An activity without ownership requires as its counterpart a perverse form of passivity. For one could, after all, imagine passivity in quite another way. Passivity is by no means inherently antithetical to sexual desire or pleasure—quite the contrary, if the level of stimulation is appropriate and can be contained. And one might likewise ask why subjectivity should not be allied with passivity—or for that matter, with being adored and admired, the subject/object of someone else's narcissism, their partner in a mutual identificatory love. Can't passivity be enjoyed without relinquishing all claim to activity, without becoming simply the active lover's object, being rather a subject who owns the pleasure of each position?

Freud's schema implies that the position of receiving stimulation, holding tension (aggressive or sexual) or directing it inward is unpleasure. That the thing to do is to push out, not take in. This implies a particular version of passivity, a traumatic experience of passivity as overstimulated helplessness or longing in abandonment. It implies not just lack or absence, but absence of a containing other in the face of overwhelming tension, the unmanageable excitement of unfulfilled desire whose object is uncertain, evasive, impregnable. This version of passivity is ultimately associated with masochism, the inward-turning of sexuality and aggression; it refers to a relation of doer and done to in which each can play only one part, and hence, a relation of domination built upon splitting. Insofar as this defense against helplessness creates and defines femininity, Freud's women appear to be faced with the choice of masochism or renunciation of desire.

Thus, the problem of woman's elusive desire brings up yet again the question with which we began, What does it mean to be a subject, in particular a subject of desire? In the past, writing on woman's desire (Benjamin, 1986a; 1986b; 1988), I suggested that understanding woman's desire might help us to reformulate our notion of subjectivity, sexual subjectivity in particular. Reflecting on thoughts of Winnicott (1971), I suggested that sexual subjectivity requires not only the drive, which has been signified as masculine, but the container, signified as feminine; not only the identification with the active father but also with the active mother, and so with the sense of authorship, which relates to functions signified as feminine and maternal like interiority, containment, being with the other. We might contend that sexual subjectivity is constituted as much by being able to *own* desire, contain excitement, hold it (metaphorically speaking) "inside" the body rather than evacuating it immediately through discharge. Indeed, all traditions of erotic wisdom value this capacity to hold excitement in the body. Discharge into the other, though ostensibly active, is properly speaking reactive, lacking the ownership that should characterize the act of a subject—a subject who could find pleasure with another subject. The fact that this defensive stance, endemic to masculinity as we know it, was so easily conflated with subjectivity should not surprise us.

This defensive activity, which aspires to self-sufficient completeness and control over the object, has been located by Breen in the position organized in terms of the phallus rather than the penis. The alternate position, in her view, is that of "penis as link" in which the vagina is known and linking between two bodies is possible. Although Breen conceives of this as an oedipal position, I suggest that it fits better with the postoedipal symbolic position as Bassin (1997) and I have described it. Indeed, I would put more emphasis than Breen on the alternative conception of active holding in the symbolization of the vagina. However, Breen's formulations have led me to rethink my argument in *The Bonds of Love*, in which I maintained that the vagina could not be used to counter the phallus in symbolizing woman's desire because it would be occurring on the same symbolic level in which the phallus is hegemonic. Rather, I proposed, we might think of woman's desire in terms of the use of inner space to represent the intersubjective space between self and other. I would now say that in the postoedipal position of symbolic activity the vagina can function symbolically to represent that space in which the union between two subjects/bodies occurs. The holding function of the vagina can be seen as related to a spacial metaphor of encompassing twoness, active holding (Bernstein, 1990), rather than merely a passive container. (NB: I say "can," because I do not think that the genital organs are privileged over other body parts, especially the body as whole in the capacity to hold excitement, although they have obviously accumulated great representational powers).

In transcending the oedipal polarity of active-passive, not only is the phallus converted into the symbolic penis, but the vagina attains the status of postoedipal symbol. The vagina can represent the quality of ownership, of containing one's desire and excitement, without which active subjectivity is thinned to a defensive construct. The holding of excitment also refers to the mother before the oedipal split into phallic and receptive, when she combined structure, regulation and recognition. Thus the metaphor of holding, the ownership of desire, transcends gender polarity and returns us to gender ambiguity. It follows that another aspect of this symbolization of woman's sexuality, which contributes to overcoming the defensive construction of activity, is a conception of the mother as a desiring subject (as mentioned in Chapter 1). This, in turn, relies on a conception of woman as not necessarily mother, but owning multiple positions and relations—a view of the mother, that does not derive from the mother-baby dyad. By this I mean a mother who could actively desire the father or any other not as a display of feminine passivity but her ownership of desire, not as a repetition of the move from omnipotence to a castrated condition.

Once we question the splitting of the mother into those two polarized positions, we are able to formulate another image of subjectivity. In this image, the formal elements of the complementary opposition, like taking in and putting out, become less antithetical, more oscillating and alternating. In this way, the effort to reclaim women's subjectivity, with its initial act of reversal in favor of a feminine holding, begins to transform the notion of what it means to be a subject. This transformation makes authorship as important as agency, and defines it in a way that allows for receiving rather than merely expressing, owning as well as expelling. Like the overinclusive identifications with maternal and paternal, the coexistence of these formerly split elements in a tension that can hold activity and passivity is crucial to a subjectivity that can love another subject. A subjectivity that owns as well as acts can—some of the time—say with Whitman "the other I am must not abase itself to you, And you must not be abased to the other."

3
The Shadow of the Other Subject
Intersubjectivity and Feminist Theory

> The result was not the normal one of a withdrawal of the libido
> from this object and a displacement of it on to a new one . . . the
> free libido was not displaced on to another object; it was with-
> drawn into the ego. There, however, it was not employed in any
> unspecified way, but served to establish an identification of the
> ego with the abandoned object. Thus the shadow of the object
> fell upon the ego. . . .
>
> —Freud, 1917

It is well understood that Freud's development of a theory of identification was a momentous step in understanding how the apparent boundaries of the self are actually permeable, how the
apparently isolated subject constantly assimilates what is outside itself. The implications of this realization are manifold, but we might
say this otherness casts a shadow on the ego from two directions:
The ego is not really independent and self-constituting, but is actually made up of the objects it assimilates; the ego cannot leave the
other to be an independent outside entity, separate from itself, because it is always incorporating the other, or demanding that the
other be like the self. From these points follow two distinct interpretations of the idea that the self is nonidentical. First, the self is
constituted by the identifications with the other that it deploys in
an ongoing way, in particular to deny the loss and uncontrollability
that otherness necessarily brings. Second, it is reciprocally constituted in relation to the other, depending on the other's recognition,
which it cannot have without being negated, acted on by the other,
in a way that changes the self, making it nonidentical. While both
ideas reveal the self's dependency on the other, only the second
takes the intersubjective view of the other as more than the self's
object.

An intersubjective theory of the self is one that poses the question of how and whether the self can actually achieve a relationship to an outside other without, through identification, assimilating or being assimilated by it. This question—how is it possible to recognize an other?—may be taken as another aspect of the problem addressed by much feminist writing: From what position is it possible to respect difference, or rather multiple differences? That discussion of difference has been closely tied to the questioning of the subject (Smith, 1988), which has raised certain objections to the very notion of recognition that is central to intersubjective theorizing. These objections, I will suggest, ought to be adressed for they will serve to clarify a psychoanalytic theory of intersubjectivity. The need for this challenge is evident when we consider the tendency in psychoanalytic writing to label intersubjective all interaction involving two persons (Stolorow & Atwood, 1984), while ignoring the difference between the subject's relationship to others and objects (Benjamin, 1995a).

The form of this challenge to the philosophical notion of subjectivity serves to differentiate poststructural thought from earlier critical theory (that associated with the Frankfurt school in particular), and seemingly led to a schism between them. Since I find that this schism, which in some respects parallels the division between Lacanian and relational feminists, results in an unproductive characterization of both sides, I shall try to bring these viewpoints into a productive confrontation, a negotiation of differences. I shall begin by referring to a debate among feminist philosophers (Benhabib, Butler, Cornell, & Fraser, 1995), putting it to use to clarify issues I believe vital to an intersubjectively conceived psychoanalysis. Before doing so, let me briefly orient my psychoanalytic readers who may be less familiar with the terms of this debate.

French philosophy and social theory, in particular the deconstruction and poststructural theory of the sixties and seventies, became so influential in North America by the eighties that they arguably established the main discursive connections in feminist thought and cultural theory. Although it is not my intent here to make hash of the differences in these schools of thought (Butler, 1990), certain ideas emerged from that matrix which shaped many discussions within feminist theory and cultural studies in Britain and North America, leading to debates about postmodernism and feminism (Flax, 1990; Nicholson, 1990). A central theme in this matrix has been the critique of essentialism (Fuss, 1989), of any attempt to secure the normative foundations of political inclusion and individual autonomy by reference to the nature of the subject, history, etc. This challenge superceded and indeed faulted the neo-Marxist, Freudian critique of the autonomous individual thinking subject such as one finds in modernist critical theory like that of the Frankfurt School. It claimed that the neo-Marxist Freudian critique was content to reveal the material, social interdependency and unconscious *nature* that underlies the apparent discreteness of the bourgeois subject, but still retained nature as an ultimate locus of authority. For example, in the work of Marcuse, sexuality assumes the place of nature as that which is repressed by civilization, much like it does for Freud. But in that of the poststructuralist Foucault, nature and sexuality are not uncovered by psychoanalysis, they are rather produced by modern discourse (Martin, 1982; Rajchman, 1991). From this perspective, one could say that the modernist critiques also reasserted essentialism by allowing the "social" or "history" to occupy the same essential, universalizing place that had formerly been occupied by nature. In this sense, the Marxian idea of the working class as a universal subject of a universal history with a defined telos could now be seen as an attempt to invent "second nature." This centered subject of history or critical theory simply displaced, while preserving its formal position and attributes, the autonomous individual that liberal theory situated in the state of nature.

Particularly significant for feminist theory was Lacan's (1988) argument that the Cartesian consciousness was overthrown by Freud's notion of the unconscious but was reintroduced by ego psychology—a Copernican revolution followed by a North American counterrevolution. The pivotal step beyond modernist theory and away from this emancipatory, humanistic concept of the ego consisted of the structural, linguistic turn: establishing that the subject is a position produced in language, not a signifier that refers to the actual mind of a person. Through a process of mutual assimilation between psychoanalysis and modern French theory, the objection to a pregiven subject was grafted onto the phenomenology of the self or psyche as well. For Lacan, the linguistic turn made it possible both to situate the subject in language, indeed to see "him" as subjected, and to reject the notion of identity or unity of the ego. Arguing that the division between conscious and unconscious in modernist psychoanalytic thought did not secure psychoanalysis against a notion of a unitary ego, Lacan's position defines the ego as created in alienation, irrevocably split (Lacan, 1977a).

While Lacan's attack on the idea of a unitary ego scarcely affected its target, North American ego psychology, it has deeply imbued feminist thought. Thus arose another point of intense disagreement between feminist object relations theory and a large body of feminist theory oriented to Lacan, deconstruction, and poststructuralism. But whereas that disagreement seemingly defined the feminist psychoanalytic debates in the 1980's, much has since changed. Despite the obvious divergences that separate relational psychoanalysis from Lacanian and poststructural thought, this challenge to the centered subject has found resonance among many relational psychoanalysts. Influenced by feminist thought (Rivera, 1989) and social constructivism (see Hoffman, 1991), relational analysts posed a related challenge to the idea of the unitary self and the objective, knowing subject of classical psychoanalysis (Aron, 1996; Bromberg, 1993; Dimen, 1995; Hoffman, 1991; Mitchell, 1993; Stern, 1992). It now seems particularly pertinent to query the usefulness of the old way of formulating the theoretical oppositions that arose from the postmodern challenge to the subject. I shall therefore take up some of the issues that have been raised by feminists influenced by Lacanian and poststructural thought, working from my own relational feminist position with roots in critical theory.

Perhaps what most distinguishes my viewpoint from the feminist fusion of French theorizing is that I have emphasized the question of recognizing the concrete other whereas they have focused on the deconstruction of the split subject as dispersed or decentered. But it seems, as I have said, that the two positions might fruitfully interact, questioning the subject while considering the problem of recognition. For this questioning has elaborated the intrinsic problem of identity or identification, that of assimilating difference. It is thus implicitly linked to the problem of recognizing the different other. I shall begin by recalling the debate between Benhabib and Butler (Benhabib, 1992; Benhabib, Butler, Cornell, & Fraser, 1995), which might appear to move along the lines of schism between critical theory and poststructuralism, and to a lesser degree, object relations and Lacanian theory.

Benhabib (1992a), who is allied with the tradition of critical theory, the later works by Habermas in particular, takes aim at some of the postulates of "the postmodern position," among which the challenge to the subject is central.[1] Benhabib objects to the "strong version" of the formulation that the subject is an effect of discourse, suggesting instead a "weak version" of the thesis, that "would situate the subject in the context of various social, linguistic and discursive practices." She hopes thereby to save the "traditional attributes of the philosophical subject of the West, like self-reflexivity, the capacity for acting on principles . . . in short, some form of autonomy and rationality"(214). She wants to argue that "the subject is not reducible to 'yet another position in language,' " but has the autonomy to "rearrange the significations of language." Otherwise, says Benhabib, it would not be possible to maintain as Butler does that the subject can be constituted by language and yet not be determined by it.

In arguing this, Benhabib raises the crucial objection to the poststructural position: Does the structuring of the I by language and cultural codes not bypass the question "what mechanisms and dynamics are involved . . . *how* the human infant becomes the social self, regardless of the cultural and normative content which defines selfhood"(217). This distinction between the subject and self is crucial. But in a more problematic vein, Benhabib outlines a notion of self that may not be sufficiently distinct from that of the philosophical subject, not sufficiently problematic. She asks if we are able to "articulate a sense of self better than the model of autonomous individuality with fluid ego boundaries and not threatened by otherness?" And here Benhabib's reference to *The Bonds of Love* implies that this is my position as well. But, as I tried to emphasize there and subsequently, negation is an equally vital moment in the movement of recognition. Nor can any appeal to the acceptance of otherness afford to leave out the inevitable breakdown of recognition into

---

[1] Part of this debate centers around the question of whether one could, as Benhabib applying a scheme proposed by Flax (1990) does, legitimately sum up the postmodern position into a set of theses about "the death of man, the death of history and the death of metaphysics." Butler takes strong exception to this synthesis, on the ground that it reduces stark differences between theorists, e.g. the poststructuralism of Foucault, the deconstruction of Derrida, the feminist psychoanalytic work of Irigaray, the cultural theory of Lyotard. Originally published in the journal *Praxis*, the papers are now available separately (Benhabib (1992 a & b), Butler (1992) and with comments by Fraser and Cornell in a volume *Feminist Contentions* (1995).

domination.[2] Benhabib's formulation seems to avoid the well-known objection, raised not only by Butler, that recognition itself can go over the edge into knowledge as mastery (Hegelian synthesis). To articulate the conditions for recognizing the other, we must understand the deepest obstacles within the self, and acknowledge that this ideal of autonomous knowing reason has served to obscure those dynamics, if not, indeed, to foster them.

Butler (1992) replies to Benhabib that power is always implicated in both authorizing certain speakers as subjects and excluding others, that discourse already constructs the positions that the subject takes, even the ones opposed by the subject. The hypothetical "I," and even Butler herself, "would not be a thinking, speaking 'I' if not for those positions . . . [since even the positions] that claim that the subject must be given in advance, that discourse [must be] an instrument or reflection of that subject, are already part of what constitutes me." Butler contends that her position does not eliminate agency but clarifies its conditions. The determination of the subject, the fact that it is constituted over and over again, is a way of recognizing the "very precondition of its agency" and thus to deconstruct the subject is "not to negate or to dismiss" it, only to expose the concealed authority and acts of exclusion behind the subject. The upshot of her argument is that "no subject can be its own point of departure" (9–15). The autonomy and intact reflexivity that Benhabib wants to rescue have been revealed to be an illusion, based on the denial of the subject's social production, as well as on a break that conceals and represses what constitutes it. As feminist theory has shown, the subject, more precisely the historically masculine subject, has always been constituted by its disavowal of dependency on the maternal, the subordination and control of what it needs.

---

[2]Actually, Benhabib and Butler seem to agree in their view of what the object relations feminist position entails, although they disagree on its value: a balance between "autonomous justice thinking and empathetic care" (Benhabib) or an "androgynous resolution" of a "unified self" which integrates "nurturance and dependency into the masculine sphere . . . autonomy into the feminine" (Butler, 1990). This strikes me as a simplification in regard to my work, which aims to deconstruct autonomy and show that these oppositions are traceable to a split pursuant on the paradoxical condition that we are dependent for recognition of our independence, and to the repudiation of the original other / mother upon whom this dependence devolves.

Fraser (1995), in her comments on the debate, rightly suggests that one does not have to choose between critical theory or postmodernism, that this opposition leads to false antinomies. Rather, each can help to clarify the problems in the other, even as Butler and Benhabib each expose the weaknesses of the other's argument. Butler collapses self and subject, as if political, epistemological positions, such as the "identity" of women as a unified political subject, fully correspond to the psychological concept of the self. To the extent that she defines emancipation as liberation from identity she also finds the problem of the other less interesting than the problem of identity. This tendency, perhaps endemic to critiques of identity, may perpetuate an elision between the other whom we create through our own identifications and the concrete outside other. But Fraser poses the crucial problem in Benhabib's return to the idea of the autonomous subject, which in effect falls short of her own arguments elsewhere (Benhabib, 1992b) that autonomy is itself a discursive ideal, one based on exclusion and domination of the other, within and without.

But I think this challenge to the autonomous subject requires more than deconstruction of the old notion of a centered unified self. I agree with Benhabib that it requires a notion of an inclusive subjectivity that can assume multiple positions and encompass the Other within. In contrast to Benhabib, I emphasize the negative: that omnipotence is and has always been a central problem for the self, disavowed rather than worked through by its position as rational subject. In fact, if the other were not a problem for the subject, the subject would again be absolute—either absolutely separate or assimilating the other. Therefore, the negativity that the other sets up for the self has its own possibilities, a productive irritation, heretofore insufficiently explored.

A further danger of the rationalist appeal to the notion of the reasoning subject is that it excludes from itself the violence and horror of which we are capable. That is, it excludes unreason. As Bataille (1991) (not unlike Adorno, 1966) proposed in his remarks on a memoir of Auschwitz, the critique of the subject need not deny reason, but it must grasp its negative moment. Thus, in his reflections on the concentration camps, Bataille (1991) points to the problem of positioning the excluded other of reason as that which alone exposes the truth. He suggests rather that "reason brings about in and of itself that which the irrational does from the outside: its own endless questioning . . . . the doubt that awakening is. Only what would this awakening be . . . if it did not awake first to the possibility of Auschwitz, to the potential for stench and unalleviated fury?" Bataille expatiates on the use of moral rationalism to suppress the full extent of horror: "There exists in a certain form of moral condemnation an escapist denial. One says, basically, this abjection would not have been, had there not been monsters . . . one subtracts the monsters from the possible. One implicitly accuses them of exceeding the limit of the possible . . . " (15–19). This possible self, this monster, must be included in any conception of the self that intends to confront that violence to the other, the revulsion at which motivates the appeal to respect, recognition, of difference.

Psychoanalytically, we associate violence with the problem of omnipotence. By omnipotence, we mean not merely a wish, but a mental state, generally understood as one of undifferentiation. In this state we are unable to take in that the other person does not want what we want, do what we say. Paradoxically, however, the self may be invested in depositing its repudiated aspects in the other, using it to represent what is despised or intolerable—for instance, weakness or aggression—and so necessarily casts the other in the role of opposite (see Altman, 1995). Violence is the outer perimeter of the less dramatic tendency of the subject to force the other to either be or want what it wants, to assimilate the other to itself or make it a threat. It is the extension of reducing difference to sameness, the inability to recognize the other without dissolving her/his otherness (Irigaray, 1985).

The query into the obligation or possibility of sustaining respect for difference without reducing the other to the same—"the ethical question"—has emerged as a logical counterpart to the question of the subject (Cornell, 1992). Such a query obliges us to avoid the ultimate escapism of moralism, of denying the monster, the Other, within. This is the danger common not only to the defenses of the rational subject but also theories of exclusion that make identification with the outside Other into an unquestioned position of the "good." Therefore, the difficulty I wish to address regarding the subject relates as much to the typical reversal it spawns as to itself. I believe such reversals are inevitable and unproductive unless we are aware of the psychic structure that underlies them.

If an emphasis on the production of the subject as a position in discourse overrides consideration of the psychological production of the self, it is not possible to ask the question of what allows the self to respect difference. Any number of theorists, not merely those like Benhabib who come from the direction of critical theory, have taken up the issue of eliminating social agency from the "subject," (Smith, 1988; Flax, 1990) but my concern here is with the elimination of psychic agency (Mahoney & Yngvesson, 1992): the disregard of motivation, need, or desire, which are inextricable from the concrete other, who not only constructs but responds to need or desire.[3] To be sure, the psychological notion of the self has its limits just as the idea of the subject of discourse has: Either notion will, if used to displace the other, become falsely totalizing.

But if the idea of "the doer behind the deed," (see Butler, 1990) an agent or self that precedes the act, is rejected, the psychological relations that constitute the self collapse. They become indistinguishable from the epistemological and political positions that constitute the subject of knowledge or history. Take Butler's use of the objection that the "I" is a grammatical fiction derived from the statement "I think"—that instead things, thoughts, feelings "come to me" (Butler, 1990, 21). It aims at the self-originating philosophical ego but misses the psychoanalytic concept of self. A psychoanalytical conception of the self always includes what "comes to me," even if felt to be alien. It is necessarily composed of such otherness, if only at the schizoid level, in which the self's experience appears as "it" rather than as "I" (Ogden, 1986). The self may or may not experience thoughts as coming from "outside," or "inside," and may in so doing own them and acknowledge its own division.

Butler's main assertion in *Gender Trouble*, that there is no gender identity "behind" expressions of gender, is clarifying, reminding us that gendered positions are multiple, nonidentical. But identity is not self. Self is a category distinct from that of identity. We can say that a self can be nonidentical, and yet contain a state, express a feeling, identify with or assume a position. The critique of identity does not prevent us from postulating a psychic subjectivity that takes up various positions through identification, a kind of "identifier behind the identification." Consider Butler's (1993a) statement that "the forming of a subject requires an identification with the normative phantasm of 'sex,' and this identification takes place through a repudiation which produces a domain of abjection." We see it is possible to write

---

[3] By "concrete other" I do not mean the opposite of the "generalized other" in Benhabib's (1995b) sense, the particular, historical individual with needs, but rather the phenomenological, "real" other in contradistinction to the abstract other. The abstract other is always constituted as the negation of the subject, as woman is Other to man; and this abstract other parallels the psychoanalytic split-off other who represents an unwanted or disowned part of self. The distinction between the concrete and abstract other is the basis for the distinction I will emphasize between the outside other and the intrapsychic object, the Other within.

of the subject in a wholly passive voice, as something that is formed, produced by an exclusionary matrix, whose sex will be materialized, and this will all be done through "the regulation of identificatory practices." There is no self that does the identifying in this text.

Oddly, Butler's (1990, 1995) use elsewhere of Freud's notion of melancholy in the formation of identifications seems to rely on a self that identifies, as in object relations theory. In this text, however, Butler postulates a discursively produced dichotomy between a world of subjects and abjects, the latter formed through exclusion. While this discourse analysis does not preclude a use of the concept of identification, it does seemingly ignore the fact that both groups require psychological selves, that both identify or disidentify with their place. Again, the political position of subject or abject must be understood as distinct from the notion of a self who may take up either or both positions. Otherwise one fails to ask how and why, dynamically, a self excludes something that is felt to be dangerous, makes it abject—an operation that Kristeva (1986), and in other terms, Theweleit (1987), have explored in the relation to woman and to the origins of abjection and horror.

The operative concept involved in understanding this process — the concept of splitting—works very differently in Lacanian thinking than in object relations theory. While any rigorous psychoanalytic notion of splitting challenges the post-Cartesian view of a unitary, self-enclosed consciousness (Whitebook, 1994), Lacan's (1977b) strategy was to locate that challenge in the fact that the subject can only operate through the division and alienation language institutes. We have no access to a self prior to, not formed through, language. The purpose of his argument was thus to break up the omnipotence of the subject through this notion of its subjection, its irrevocable split. The approach of object relations psychoanalysis, by contrast, is to link omnipotence with the act of splitting as the ego's defensive act; not to say that the subject *is* split, rather that the self (or ego) *splits*, that is, engages in the activity of splitting. The notion of splitting as an active, ongoing process of psychic defense performed by the self sets up the question of the subject differently than the notion of a split subject or identity constituted by discourse, language, normative practices, or any other structures that render the subject an "effect."

The object relations viewpoint, with its roots in Kleinian theory, is that the self is constantly, dynamically engaged in acts of incorporation and projection in which parts of self and other are split off (Klein, 1946; Rosenfeld, 1971). This theory would seem to be the origin of Kristeva's (1982) idea of abjection, in which the self actively

creates the abject within the dichotomy "part-of- self" and "repudiated not-part-of-self."[4] The ability to split may be seen as endemic,
innate, a pregiven property of the mind like the ability to use language. Indeed, splitting in that sense is not only defensive but organizing; by setting boundaries and discriminating, it allows the self to
keep from being overwhelmed by bounding and discriminating
what confronts it (Ogden, 1986; Aron, 1995). Unlike the "split subject," a concept that is set up in opposition to "unity"—relying on
the falseness of its binary Other to generate its oppositional truth—
the notion of splitting does not require that we posit a preexisting
unity, or an ideal of unity to which splitting gives the lie.

Butler (1992) works with the active form of splitting when she
warns against any version of the "subject" that "disavows its consti-
tutive relations by recasting them as the domain of countervailing
externality." Here she is referring to male disavowal of the mother.
But I would maintain that such a postulate about the constitution of
the autonomous subject through the disavowal of maternal dependency unavoidably leads to a further, unstated consequence: The notion of recasting presupposes that the maternal other could have
been or could be something apart from and prior to the disavowal,
that it was and is a partner. It was, in short, once a concrete other in
a reciprocal relationship where each constitutes the other. Cornell
(Cornell, 1995) in her comment on the debate between Benhabib and
Butler, does explicate this consequence and does show how a notion
of recognizing the externality of the other might follow from Butler's position, and I shall return to her argument later.[5] Unlike Lacanian theory, which locates this relationship in the unknowable,

---

[4] Kristeva's notion of the abjected as that which is propelled out of the self,
ab-ject rather than ob-ject, refers both to a process of separation as well as
that which is separated from—principally the maternal body and the self's
remainders (e.g. feces) that become repellent through separation. See "Freud
and Love," (1986) for its use as a process of separation, and *Powers of Horror*
(1982) for the discussion of the abject as repudiated substance.

[5] Using a Lacanian framework, Cornell reaches a position similar to the one
that I see as essential to the critique of ego psychology (Benjamin, 1995a):
that the act of internalization is that by which the ego denies the alterity of
the other. Thus internalizing stands in an obverse relation to recognition; is
that which occurs when the sequence of destruction, survival, and recognition of externality fail. However, to the extent that Lacan locates (or so he is
read) the early maternal relationship outside the knowable, her point may
not be internally consistent.

prelingual domain outside history, intersubjective theory begins with the possibility and necessity of this relationship in the (partially knowable) history of the self.

Such a historicized conception of the relationship to the original other prior to its psychic and social disavowal in the oedipal repudiation of the mother has been formulated by psychoanalytic feminists as diverse as Irigaray (1991) and Chodorow (1980), in both Lacanian and object relations language. Only this presupposition of a prior erotic attachment/identification, as Butler (1990, 1995) indeed argues regarding homosexual relationships, explains that violent mental act through which a concrete other is transformed into a split off, repudiated part-self. If we return the subject to the position of self confronting an external other, actively engaging this transformation, we may then see how the shadow of the other (in contrast to the internalized object) falls upon the subject. To do this requires a distinction between the intrapsychic and intersubjective dimensions of psychoanalytic theory, not an elimination of one in favor of another. It requires upholding the double-sidedness of the relation to the other.

Let us consider the distinction between intrapsychic and intersubjective. The difference between the conception of ego and its object and that of self with other roughly parallels Winnicott's (1971) distinction between relating through identifications to the subjectively conceived object and using the externally perceived object. While acknowledging the contribution of the object to the subject, intrapsychic theory did not fully confront the subject with the outside other, with anything external to its own projections and identifications. This left the subject with nothing other than introjective-projective "web-spinning," as Eigen (1981) aptly put it. Thus despite the recognition of the relation to the object and the insight into manic defenses, intrapsychic theory did not produce a critique of the self-enclosed, independent self. In Kleinian theory, if the self can contain the tension between the positions of being good and bad, between envy and reparation, the relation to the "whole object" will follow. Alterity is not in itself formulated as a problem.

The crucial move beyond this Kleinian position was Winnicott's (1971) realization that omnipotence cannot be broken up without a process of "destruction," which may, if survived, lead to recognition of the existence of the other as external. Winnicott emphatically stated that he called it destruction because of the liability of the other not to survive. In this liability is contained the indeterminacy and irreducibility of the other for the subject. To survive is to withstand the self's act of negation— which might consist of an attack, a refusal to comply, a "You do not exist for me"—and reflect the subject's impact without retaliation or submission. The other who survives can be seen in its alterity, as external—outside one's own control and yet able to have decisive impact on the self.

In the individual history of the self, we visualize the problem of destruction arising at the point where the significant others do not survive the child's acts, but rather through punitive retaliation or failure to react, through aggression or absence, do not facilitate the emergence of feeling for and with the other. The more acute failures of survival are usually enacted at the level of the early body ego, where projection of the bad, angry self is expressed in bodily metaphor, perhaps in concrete physical disgust or real violence. Ordinary failures often are reflected at the level of language when the ego excludes, silences, and devalues the externalized bad object. When destructiveness has not been survived but met with punishment by a "moral force" it is commonly internalized in the moral agency—as in Freud's (1930) description of the superego feeding on the aggression toward the "unattackable authority." The self now has a choice of fleeing or being the superego: condemning the other's evocations of unameliorated destructiveness, or identifying with them. The self thus limited in its contact with externality remains in the thrall of idealization and repudiation, of identifications and projections. These then facilitate or even require submission to an authority or redeemer, or (to bring in the matter of identity) subjection to a "moral" identity set up to oppose the externalized, bad object.

From the concept of survival follows a distinction crucial in psychoanalytic practice: that between transference-countertransference based on projective identification, in which the other is only felt to embody part of self, and (un)conscious communication based on mimetic resonance, in which two separate minds are felt to be present (Sandler, 1993). For Winnicott's final conclusion is that only the outside other can be loved. It is ultimately this pleasure in the discovery of somebody to love that compensates the break up of identity. And, as Winnicott added, there is always the problem of waste disposal. For it is possible to remain in self-enclosed web-spinning, to rely on the superego to contain destructiveness (not without mentally attacking the self object, to be sure). But only the concrete outside other can break up the closed energy system, only the other who can be moved but not coerced by us can take on some of what is too much for the self to bear. There is no question that we need the other—the question is only, can we recognize her? And, has not the master-slave problematic made clear to us that her otherness becomes vitiated if we fail to do so? (Benjamin, 1988)

What about the objection to recognition, on the grounds that it falsifies the difficulties of difference? Contrary to those who find in this call for recognition of the concrete other/mother a myth of harmonious reconciliation (Scott, 1993), I will suggest how the intersubjective emphasis on the relation to the outside other expands the critique of identity as it has been developed in both critical theory and postmodern feminist thought. The critique of identity has often been reiterated in feminist thought as part of the rejection of essentialism (Smith, 1988). It has been formulated in Lacanian terms, for example, by Gallop: ". . . any identity will necessarily be alien and constraining. But I do not seek some liberation from identity. That would lead to another form of paralysis—the oceanic passivity of undifferentiation. Identity must be continually assumed and immediately called into question" (Gallop, 1982). This position recapitulates Adorno's critique of identification and identity, his excoriations of the absolute subject. Adorno was concerned to show how the act of knowing aimed to assimilate the other completely into itself. Thus he speaks of "the totality of the concept, the absolute domination of the subject":

> The circle of identification, that finally only identifies with itself, is drawn by the thought that tolerates nothing outside; its imprisonment is its own handiwork. . . . Even the theory of alienation, ferment of the dialect, confuses the need to come close to the heteronomous and thereby irrational world . . . with the archaic barbarism of the longing subject that is not capable of loving the alien, the other; with the greedy thirst for incorporation and persecution. (1966, 172)

Adorno's effort to unseat identity finally could only offer the continual negation through self-reflection. And this position, whether in its critical theory or later deconstructionist versions, has been most assiduous in exposing the absolutism of the thinking subject, the domination inherent in the process of identification. However, Adorno's critique of the subject remained constrained by his view of the object, which was never formulated intersubjectively

(Benjamin, 1977). In the absence of intersubjectivity, the subject of re-flection can only reflect upon itself, not account for the possible transformation made by the intervention of an other whose negativity is fully independent of the subject. Habermas, on the other hand, recognized this problem and formulated an idea of intersubjectivity close to that of Mead, based on self-reflection in the third person and situated in speech interaction. However, Habermas does not allow that intersubjectivity returns us to the liability of the other not to survive, the inevitable failure of recognition. His notion of internal-izing the other's position does not distinguish externality from iden-tificatory assimilation of the other (see Habermas, 1992). In fact, neither Adorno nor Habermas succeeded in elaborating a position of recognition or reflection that takes us "beyond" the superego.

On balance, in considering the well-known line-up of Haber-mas *v.* Adorno, we might say that whereas Adorno bequeathed us the critique of identity without intersubjectivity, Habermas provided an entry into intersubjectivity, but without sufficient attention to the subject's destructive omnipotence. In this case, a synthesis seems tempting. But it is not my intent to discuss their two theories in de-tail. Here I merely want to emphasize that the adumbration of inter-subjectivity must continually retain the awareness of the other's liability not to survive. It therefore cannot dispense with the critique of identity, which addresses the self where survival fails, in the in-trapsychic enclosure of identification and projection. The embrace of intersubjectivity does not constitute a transcendence (*Aufhebung*) of the intrapsychic, but rather a modification and addition to it (Ben-jamin, 1995a).

But this modification is crucial. The intersubjective idea of negation is especially relevant to those who, even as they embrace the critique of identity, seek a way out of the dilemma posed by it. Who accept the premise of a nonunified, constructed subject but do not want to leave the subject merely decentered and dispersed. At-tempting to get beyond the impasses proceeding from the decon-struction of the subject, such critics (de Lauretis, 1986; Smith, 1988) propose that the subject's agency and liberation derive from iden-tity's very negativity, the contradictions between its multifarious po-sitions. The notion of agency can, in this view, be rescued by locating its source in the clash of culturally instituted subject positions—an argument Butler (1992) seems to make as well. But, even if this were so, agency is not the only thing to be rescued from our critique of the subject. And so I would argue that it still remains necessary to articulate the indispensable negativity provided by the other, alongside the negativity within. In order to go beyond a conception of a self-enclosed self, to recuperate difference and respect for otherness along with agency, we have to account for the impact of the other on the self. This impact provides a negation that is at once indeterminate and irreducible to the subject's own mental world, thus not the subject's own constructed, internal Other, even though related and interdependent with it.

The psychoanalytic formulation of the question of the other corresponds to the "ethical question" to which poststructural and deconstructionist thought have recurred (see Bernstein, 1992; Cornell, 1992). Cornell (1995) draws the link this way: "The beginning of the other subject demands the recognition that Woman is Other to the fantasy structures of the masculine psyche. Thus there is an ethical and a political meaning for feminism in the recognition of the externality of the other." This recognition by the subject of his reproduction which "follows" the other/mother is "not the death of the subject but the 'birth' of a subject other for the ego" (154). Here again the necessity of conceiving a being external and given to the subject: Only thus can we make a distinction between locating the other as a disowned part of the self (fantasy other) in a complementary opposition and recognizing the "real" concrete other/mother who has preceded us, whom we require. (Indeed, necessarily mother and father precede us, so that mother's desire comes before our own.)

The question of recognition is also, as Cascardi (1992) suggests, always the question of whether there will be peace or war, a struggle to triumph and annihilate or a negotiation of difference. The question—Can a subject relate to the other without assimilating the other to the self through identification?—corresponds to the political question, Can a community admit the Other without her/him having to already be or become the same? What psychoanalysis considers the problem of overcoming omnipotence is thus always linked to the ethical problem of respect and the political of problem of nonviolence.

It is worth considering what we mean by omnipotence, and whether it is necessary to posit it as a kind of primordial condition (see the discussion of Stern & Pine in Benjamin, 1988). If omnipotence is asserted only in the moment when the self recognizes the possible threat that the other poses, we see that otherness and omnipotence are always mutually constituting. Omnipotence is only known retroactively, when it no longer is such. Only in the moment of constituting a separate I (for myself) can the other threaten it—

even when, in fact, I am constituted for an other, and this constitution is called in question by a second other. The moment in which omnipotence is continually recharged is that of facing the fact of dependency on others outside our control. Of course, this confrontation extends beyond the need for loved others to the world at large. Merely by living in this world, we are exposed to others and subjected to unconscious, unwilling identification with others (on television, if not begging on the streets). Whether we will or no, the world exposes us to the *different* others who, not only in their mere existence as separate beings reflect our lack of control, but who also threaten to evoke in us what we have repudiated in order to protect the self: weakness, vulnerability, decay, or perhaps sexual otherness, transgression, instability—the excluded abject in either Kristeva's and Butler's sense. It is not truly in our power not to identify; what we cannot bear to own, we can only repudiate.

In yet another sense we are captive to identification, for recognition inevitably takes the indirect and potentially alienating form of identification, in which self takes the other as ideal or as a part of self, thus abrogating difference and externality.[6] The object may be assimilated as like or opposite, taking the form of the split unity, in which self and other are assigned complementary parts that can be switched, but never held together. But the way out of these identificatory processes is not merely escape into the superego, whose moral condemnation may be used to counter idealization or repudiations; nor through simple identification with or revaluing of the despised half of the complementarity, the done to, which creates new moral imperatives, a new normativity. Identification can serve as a means for bridging difference without denying or abrogating it, but the condition of this form of identification is precisely the other's externality. The other's difference must exist outside; not be felt as a coercive command to "become" the other, and therefore not be defended against by assimilating it to self. It is here that the notion of recognition as mediated not only through identification, but

---

[6] Identification may function as ratification of sameness (merger, or potentially chauvinism, as in identity politics), as incorporation of the other whom one has lost or can lose because she is outside (ego as the precipitate of abandoned object relations), and identification with difference in which the subject struggles to become "like" what is different to be closer to it (relation to the ideal). Each of these blocks the acknowledgement of the externality of the other.

through direct confrontation with the other's externality, makes a difference.

Only the externality of the other that survives destruction allows a representation of the other as simultaneously outside control and nonthreatening—a form of negation that social relations of domination enforced by violence intrinsically prevent. The loss of externality plunges the self into unbearable aloneness, or escape into merger with like-self beings, creating an identity that demands the destructive denial of the different. I have suggested that the early developmental route out of projective-introjective assimilation turns out to be through recognition's opposing term, negation, which has to be revalued. Thus, I elaborated on Winnicott's notion of destruction—the mental refusal to recognize the other, the negation of the external—and contended that recognition practically, psychically depends upon symbolic processing of destruction.

This transposition of terms, such that recognition now depends upon negation, momentarily reverses the terms in favor of negation. But this move, in turn, makes the tension between negation and recognition dependent upon the recognition of the negation, of the other's impact or intent. For example, in the psychoanalytic framework, we understand the necessity of catching, receiving, and holding the patient's negation. Thus, negation can only be revalued as a more equal term within the context of recognition itself as the superordinate value that enables negation to have impact. It is when negation, as destruction, is not survived that it explodes this superordinate function; it is when the other is not able to change or recognize the effect, but only deflects, attacks, or withdraws (the other is "destroyed") that we can speak of the breakdown of recognition, which is not equivalent to mere negation.

The opposition recognition/negation is therefore not precisely the same opposition as mutual recognition/breakdown. The first tension can exist within the second. All negotiation of difference involves negation, often leading to partial breakdowns which we might call disruption. Breakdown, full rupture, is only catastrophic when the possibility of reestablishing the tension between negation and recognition is foreclosed, when the survival of the other for the self, of self for other, is definitely over. By the same token, recognition does not require a full reconciliation, least of all an "extorted" one, as Adorno termed it, but rather something that is both "tensed and unstable—never quite *aufgehoben* or reconciled" (Bernstein, 1992).

The complementary opposite to breakdown should not be seen as an original constancy or tension, a "steady state." It might, as has been done in the study of infant interaction, more properly be conceptualized as repair of disruption (Tronick, 1989). However, the danger of repair lies in creating false unity, which in turn will inevitably inspire breakdown, the unleashing of aggression against it. Conversely, fear of the aggression that is unleashed in breakdown may lead to the stabilization of complementarity, to "false reconciliations" whose stuckness prevents a real dialectic of breakdown and repair. The experience of repair can retroactively light up destruction's creative, differentiating side, which has the effect of placing the other in a space outside coercive reconciliation. Without the recognition of negation, there is only the false closure of contradiction, the defensive assumption of identity that conceals the real strain of acknowledging the other. Acceptance of this strain is a condition of acknowledgement, not an invalidation of it. In fact, we have reason to believe that repeated experiences of breakdown and repair result in the subject's confidence in the possibility of reinstituting tension after breakdown (Beebe & Lachman, 1994). This confidence is what allows her/him to relinquish ossified forms of complementarity, to risk the negotiation of difference (see Pizer, 1992). In this light, splitting and breakdown can be seen as a necessary moment of destructiveness to break up what is calcified (Eigen, 1993).

Further, we might recognize that alienated forms of complementarity, based on the idealization and repudiation created by splitting, are inevitable. In the best of circumstances, these alternate with recognition. It follows that the ability to symbolically work and play with the fantasmatic relations produced by splitting will be a condition of reinstituting recognition.[7] Splitting itself is not the problem, but only its rigid congelation into indissoluble complementarity, which structures the subject and his other as mirror opposites (good/bad, excluded/included). Splitting, then, need not be conceived in opposition to some normative ideal of the whole self, but rather as the initial form adopted by the self with respect to contradictions in feelings or apprehensions; it can either be transformed in relation to the outside other or reduce the other to a locus of the self's disowned parts. The point of departure for this view of split-

---

[7] This alternation of recognition and subordination is beautifully described in Ogden's (1995) discussion of the analytic third.

ting is not the self-enclosed unity of the subject, but the contradictions that our need for the other's independent existence demands
we bear.

In sum, respect for the different other requires that within the
binary hierarchy of recognition-negation, negation receives its due.
Recognition would be the "superordinate" but not the "superior"
term. Nonetheless, without positing the capacity for reciprocal recognition as one side of subjectivity, the demand to respect the different
Other (and its negative form, the objection to being silenced), has no
basis other than a problematic form of guilt, a projection of one's
own injured narcissism on to the other. Likewise, the demand to be
recognized in one's difference, raised from the position of the Other,
would have no basis other than narcissism. It reduces the ethical
question to the competition of abstract, self-interested individuals.

One of the most subtle forms of breakdown of tension occurs
when the Other is seen as exempt from the responsibilities of the
subject to deal with his/her own narcissism. As when the abused
Other makes a claim to absolute restitution by attacking the subject,
and that subject tries to flee his own guilt and preserve his own narcissism by identifying with the victim and accepting that claim. The
subject capitulates, rather than surviving with impact. This political
countertransference is like that of the analyst, working with the
abused patient, who finds herself in the role of the abused, unconsciously playing to the patient's sadistic identification with the aggressor. The analyst, in flight from her own identification with the
aggressor, accepts this reversal, is driven to make restitution for all
suffering, until she finally collapses or retaliates (Davies & Frawley,
1994). It therefore behooves the analyst to find a way to preserve her
subjectivity without counterattack, not to relinquish it in an act of
false reparation. This has been a key theme in current discussions of
relational analysis. The analyst must find some avenue to communi-
cate with the patient from one subject to another, despite the inevitable asymmetry of responsibility, for instance by controlled
aknowledgement of the patient's emotional impact (Maroda, 1995).
This implies an ongoing tension between asymmetry and mutuality
(Aron, 1996).

An historic exemplification of the breakup of exclusion, of the
self-enclosed world of the subject, might be the South African
whites' relinquishment of apartheid. The strategy of the African Na-
tional Congress exemplified the intervention of the Other as subject,
achieving through their own solidarity and recognition a form of

agency despite persecution and denial of recognition by their oppo-
nents. The ANC and Mandela assumed an ethical responsibility for
the consequences before that responsibility had been honored by the
white government, before symmetrical power had been established.
Much of what transpired in the initial transition offered an alternative to the reversal of power relations that silence the silencer. This is
the difference the Other can make, precisely because the Other insists on being a subject, not simply attacking the other's subjectivity.
We should not forget, however, that it was also De Klerck's ability to
envision *surviving* the destruction of the Afrikaner way of life that allowed difference and externality to emerge.

The notion of intersubjectivity postulates that the barbarism of
incorporating the Other into the same, the cycle of destructiveness,
can only be modified when the Other intervenes. Therefore *any subject's primary responsibility to the other subject is to be her intervening or
surviving other*. This perspective allows us to move beyond the critique of the thinking subject into the problem of identity as it presents itself in the psychopolitical world. It permits a differentiation
between the simple reversal of complementary power relations and
the concrete negation that breaks up fixed identity and allows survival—in effect, a negativity of nonviolence.

Here, indeed, is the reason it is necessary to distinguish the
subject of discourse and the self as agent. Only such a self can *own*—
assume responsibility for containing—destructiveness in self and
other rather than projecting it into the not-I or turning it against the
self. In political thinking the move to locate what is harmful in that
which constructs the subject (discourse) tends not so much to foster
awareness of subjection as to heighten the tendency to split, projecting outward what properly belongs to self.

Along with such capacity for ownership must go the capacity
for recognition. The danger of split complementarity arises if we
forgo the requirement of mutuality in recognition. Unless we accept
the formal terms of reciprocity, even in the face of asymmetry, the
critique of the subject becomes paradoxical. For then the subject is
always critiqued from the standpoint of the other who is excluded,
assimilated, unrecognized. But, I would emphasize, if this other,
who must likewise be a subject, is as incapable as the first of such
recognition, he/she is no other, but only a ruse of the subject's will
to power. To refuse this consequence is simply to split, to reverse the
complementarity, to speak from the position of the Other as "good"
and pronounce the subject "bad," thus disowning the bad subject in

ourselves. To postulate a self who can assume both "goodness" and "badness," both recognition and negation of the other, is the only ground for a critique of the subject's inability to recognize the other.

While my formulation of this position derives primarily from work within psychoanalytic theory, it turns out to correspond quite closely to the philosophical controversy between Derrida and Levinas regarding alterity (Derrida, 1978; Cornell, 1992). At issue here is whether the reduction of the other to the same is to be avoided by declaring the other to be absolutely other (Levinas), positing a radical alterity outside a knowledge which inherently strives to control it; or whether it is to be avoided by recognizing that the other must also be an alter ego, irreducible to my ego precisely because it is an ego. This issue is taken up by Derrida in his critique of Levinas's insistence on irreducible alterity: "If the other was not recognized as ego, its entire alterity would collapse" (125). The condition for the other being recognized is that the other also be a subject, an ego, capable of negating. As Cornell puts it, "The strangeness of the Other is that the Other is an 'I.' But, as an 'I,' the Other is the same as 'me.' Without this moment of universality, the otherness of the Other can be only too easily reduced to mythical projection" (57).

Reciprocity must therefore be preserved as a condition of conceiving the ethical relationship, in which, as Bernstein (1992) says, both self and other "stand under the reciprocal obligation to seek to transcend their narcissistic egoism." For "without a *mutual* recognition of this *Aufgabe* [task/obligation] of searching for commonalities and precise points of difference, without a self-conscious sensitivity of the need always to do justice to 'the other's' *singularity* . . . we are in danger of obliterating the radical plurality of the human condition" (75). I have suggested how the concept of recognition can take account of both the intrapsychic negation "within the subject" that has been elaborated against the logic of identity and the intersubjective negation of/by the other. This can be done without reconstructing a normative identity, without establishing a subject-object unity, without implying a transparent knowledge of the self or the other—these being the objections to recognition raised by feminists (Young, 1990).

It has been widely argued that, in the Hegelian concept of recognition, difference is sacrificed to recognition because both subjects are reconciled and absorbed in the higher determinations of an another form of absolute subject: *Geist*, history, the state, or community. But Cornell (1992) argues that to uphold difference also requires the preservation of Hegel's concept of recognition, with its distinction from reflection, in which the other exists simply for the self: "the protection and care of difference is not carried out to the detriment of the possibility of mutual self-recognition, if understood in the sense of the recognition of *phenomenological* symmetry" (57).

What does the protection of difference actually mean? Young (1990), in her critique of the ideal of community, argues that the notion of overcoming of otherness in mutual sympathy of reciprocal recognition upholds an ideal of homogenization in which significant differences could never be acknowledged. The other's alterity would no longer be irreducible, but fully knowable, assimilable, subject to our internalization. The notion of a transparent understanding of the other implies a transparent self, a self which does not allow the existence of its own negative, its unconscious otherness, what Kristeva called the Stranger within us. A notion of recognition as full knowing of the other, Young continues, would revive the norm of an autonomous, self-enclosed subject who always knows itself, its desires, a unity rather than heterogenous and multiple being. It would also affirm identification with commonality as *the* basis for respecting the other. This would be less likely to produce respect for otherness than chauvinism and nationalism. Or it would produce a reverse identification with the other, a self-denial that installs the excluded other in the position of the ideal.

Politically, the possibility of mutual intersubjectivity is predicated on the very difference that also leads to continual misfiring of recognition, the very plurality that strains subjectivity. Psychologically, the struggle to try to know the other while still recognizing the other's radical alterity and unknowability has to be formulated not only as one between different identities, but as disagreement and contradiction within identities. For, indeed, ideological disagreements may well override identity—not all identities think alike. Such equations between identity and thought reduce thinking itself. (One has to ask whether the notion that differences stem from identities does not repeat the perversion of Marxism according to which Leninist parties attributed challenging ["deviationist"] ideas to the ["objective"] class position of their advocates.) This requires a notion of self that need not aim at a seamless unity of consciousness by exclusion, by mistaking a part for the whole. A self that allows different voices, asymmetry, and contradiction, that holds ambivalence.

In light of these arguments, I want to take another, critical look at the theme of exclusion as it has been continually asserted in feminist thought. Here let us consider Butler's argument that subjects are necessarily created in opposition to the abject. She says, "Subjects are created through exclusion, through the creation of a domain of deauthorized subjects, presubjects, figures of abjection, populations erased from view," (Butler, 1992) or that "subjects are formed through exclusionary operations" (Scott, cited in Butler, 1992). Butler seems to posit an exclusion that has no opposing term, no *inclusion*, no formation of the subject through recognition. But if this were so, how could the "contesting and rifting" she calls for occur, how could the demand to respect difference be posed? On what basis other than an ideal of inclusion, of recognition of the other's right to participate in the polity, on what grounds—besides the sheer self-interest or power of the excluded—is exclusion to be opposed? Surely this critique of exclusion implicitly functions to make inclusion of preserved differences a normative, universal demand? And why not, as long as it remains open to interrogation?

First, let us agree that, from the standpoint of psychoanalytic theory, exclusion is a term that can only mean to psychically "relocate." Remember that a split off part of self, the internal other, is not equivalent to an external, social other who may or may not be excluded. Excluded refers to that which is repudiated, cast out of self, abjected, in order to shore up the subject's identity, not to the truly outside other. As in our representation of the universe of energy, so in that of the psychic universe the principle of conservation applies: Something that is pushed out of one psychic place ("inclusion") has to go elsewhere ("exclusion"); likewise, what one refuses to recognize outside reemerges as a dangerously threatening internal object. This internal object may then reappear "outside" as the dangerous other. It would seem, psychoanalytic theory once accepted, that we can formulate this as the essential "law of inescapability": nothing leaves our psychic universe. To deconstruct the terms by which exclusion operates, or even the opposition inclusion/ exclusion, reveals that we cannot reject exclusion without affirming inclusion, for that is a psychic impossibility.

In light of the fundamental givens of the psyche, exclusion is an illusion. The question is merely what type of inclusion we seek or flee, critique or promulgate, conceive or deny. Here our acknowledgement of the ongoing intrapsychic process of identification and projection is essential. The injunction to respect the other's external alterity, even unknowability, comes up against the problem that the *position* of the other is internal to the self (internal alterity). This position is "already" represented in the mind, either as object or other subject. This representation of the other in the self depends, in turn on certain psychic terms—love/hate, attachment/loss, life/death—which cannot be avoided, but at best can be reconfigured. As I see it, this is the position Butler (1990; 1995) takes in regard to gender identifications that become the melancholic residue of internalized prohibition: What cannot be mourned, cannot be let go, is held inside as abject, repudiated otherness. Thus, paradoxically, only inclusion, the reavowal of what was disavowed, in short *owning*, could allow that otherness a place outside the self in the realm of externality, could grant it recognition separate from self.

The challenge to the subject in terms of exclusion or identity unavoidably poses a demand for inclusion and yet that demand carries the risk of reinstituting identity, if only the identity of the Other. Indeed, it is difficult to see how a genealogy of the concept of exclusion would not find its roots in the very universal norms Butler sees as a ruse of power, as well as to the reaction spawned by those norms: The privileged position of otherness that wishes to establish a "pure" ideal, outside power. Thus I would argue that the criterion of exclusion can itself become a regulatory counterideal, establishing the position of the excluded other as a reified, indissoluble position of identity from which to attack exclusion and unmask power, as if it were free of it. Likewise, the attack on universality can fuel itself through this counteridealizing zeal, drawing its power from the act of reversal.

The idea of inclusion may be parallel to the principle of recognition, which works only insofar as it continually apprehends its dependency on negation, the breakup of identity. Only by apprehending its own inevitable failure—the ongoing tendency toward splitting, toward negation of the other, toward exclusion—can recognition of the other function. The same could be said of inclusion. The dangers of normativity, including the creations of ideals of self and other that are potentially punitive and exclusive, are evident. But these dangers cannot be avoided by repressing the idealizing, normalizing tendencies of the mind: the self's inevitable involvement in identificatory processes that foster idealization and exclusion, splitting of good and bad. Butler's use of the idea of exclusion as a touchstone seems to imply that it can function unproblematically, as if it did not rest upon another ideal, susceptible to idealization and deployment as power. But why should it not be susceptible? We may agree that, as she herself suggests (Butler, 1993b) in her discussion of Cornell's *Philosophy of the Limit*, the point is not to dispense with the ideal, but to accept the failures and losses attendant upon any relationship to ideals, the necessary tension of the difference between the ideal and the real.

Butler asks how we are to distinguish the "valorization of infinite striving" based on accepting that tension and those failures from the slave morality that uses this relation to the ideal to reinstitute a sense of failure and turn the will-to-power back on the self. What, in other words, is the difference between a philosophy of the limit and a philosophy of the superego, between a mourning that allows renewal and a melancholia that finds all political agency impossible. The main inconsistency I find in Butler's position is that she offers as worthy but unrealizable ideals Cornell's Good as a condition of the ethical relation, Laclau's emancipation as the condition of a political field mobilized by antagonisms, and her own idea of "loss of the subject as the ground of meaning" as a condition of a "discursive modality of agency." If we are able to retain ideals of the good and of emancipation, why not an ideal of an inclusive self that is the condition of multiplicity, difference and incomplete knowledge of the other? Why, when it comes to ideals, no locus of self or subjectivity, only discursivity?

Granted that inclusion is an unrealizable ideal that is worthy of our striving, it remains to establish something about the nature of a self or a polity that gives content to this ideal. Here I would like to briefly sketch an idea of the self that might hold this demand for inclusion, and yet would not require a hold in identity, which is necessarily created through exclusion. The object relations concept of self has framed the possibility of an inclusiveness without identity, a self that sustains difference and contradiction. Necessarily, however, where identity once grounded the ego, the relation to the other must now ground a self that would live without identity. For, as I said before, self does not equal identity. To include without assimilating or reducing requires us to think beyond the binary alternatives of self-enclosed identity and fragmented dispersal to a notion of multiplicity. What kind of self can sustain multiplicity, indeed, the opposition to identity that the relation with the different other brings?

Here we may see the limits of the philosophical critique of integration as a false reconciliation, which pointed out the normative problem in the psychoanalytic language of unity, coherence, identity. That critique does not speak to the concretes—fear, pain, loss—that generally drive disintegration and therefore make integration look like a good thing. The philosophical critique of the subject conflated the theoretical denial of multiplicity and discontinuity with the experience of self-continuity that Winnicott called "going on being"; it made ordinary unhappiness and neurosis indistinguishable from the anguish of "the slide into psychosis." (Flax, 1990, 219) When we move to the psychoanalytic register of the self, we change our vantage point in such a way as to focus on such experiences of anguish. To rethink integration and formulate a different notion of inclusion requires a rethinking of what the self is capable of, its catastrophes as well as its possibilities. In referring the self to its relationship with the concrete other, we locate the self in the fragile, unenclosed space of intersubjectivity, a possible reciprocity of difference and recognition, from which negativity, both creative and disastrous, cannot be excluded.

The psychoanalytic effort to replace splitting with the sustaining of psychic tension and the ability to tolerate opposing attitudes toward self and other could well stand to be freed of its legacy of normativity and advocacy for identity. But an object relations view of integrating split off aspects of self need not imply a mythical unity, a harmonious identity. To think of the self only as discursively regulated and produced would eliminate the space that includes this negativity of the self, however vital such self-reflection on the effects of regulatory discourse within psychoanalysis itself. Tolerating ambivalence, being able to feel both love and hate toward the same object, does not mean that love and hate are synthesized so that love triumphs over hate. Rather, it means that hate can be borne. Difference, hate, failure of love can be surmounted not because the self is unified, but because it can tolerate being divided. Inclusion of split off feelings or blocked aspirations is motivated not by a compulsion to restore unity but out of the wish to be less resentful and afraid of projected anger, less terrified of loss, less punitive toward what one desires.

Many contemporary relational analysts have begun to consider the importance of conceiving of a multiple rather than a unified self. Statements about the discontinuity, contradictions and multiplicity of self experience are legion in the writings of contemporary relational analysts (see Aron, Bollas, Bromberg, Davies, Eigen, Mitchell, Pizer, Rivera). But unlike the discussion in feminist theory, the psychoanalytic discussion is less preoccupied with the opposition between identity and multiplicity, for this does not adequately describe the problem of unlinked psychic states.The most interesting thinking about the use and abuse of the idea of unity has come from reflection on people who suffer from dissociated states. When experiences with the other are immediately or cumulatively traumatic, the anxiety and intolerable conflict between different reactions leads to dissociation (Davies & Frawley, 1994; Bromberg, 1995; Rivera, 1989; Schwartz, 1994; Stern, 1996). In dissociation, the awareness of transition or discrepancy between different self states is blocked. In this case we understand that the self has lost contact with its multiplicity because of dissociation—barriers to awareness erected in the face of severe pain or fear—and not because of a repression of conflict by a unified self (Rivera, 1989).

As Stephen Mitchell (1993) has contended, from a clinical standpoint both rigidity and fragmentation are equally symptomatic; the self characterized by high degrees of dissociation may appear either fragmented or rigid, chaotic or organized. To recognize high degrees of dissociation as illness is not tantamount to espousing an ideal of digestion and blending over "the capacity to contain shifting and conflictual versions of self" (105). Or as Bromberg (1993) put it, "there is no such thing as an integrated self, 'a real you.' . . . [H]ealth is not integration . . . [it] is the ability to stand in the spaces between realities without losing any of them," to replace dissociation with internal conflict (166). Thus fragmentation and multiplicity are quite different, if not to say opposed. Rivera (1989), in her discussion of dissociation and multiple personality, has argued that integration does not imply a fictional unity, but rather "the erosion of dissociative barriers to a central consciousness that can handle the contradictions of the different voices and different desires within one person . . . . not the silencing of different voices with different points of view—but the growing ability to call all those voices 'I,' to disidentify with any one of them as the whole story"(28).

The ability to disidentify is decisive for the reflexive process that makes ideals and identities separable and fluid rather than compulsory and coercive. On what is such an intrapsychic ability based? The issue cannot be discussed simply in terms of the intrapsychic ability to bring together disparate representations of the other, but also in terms of the psychoanalytic interaction that makes such a synthesis bearable. The self's ability to disidentify with any one story as the whole may appear to us as intact reflexivity, but in fact it depends upon a specific kind of *relationship* between self and other. The crux of the matter for relational theory has been to understand the way that threatening experiences necessarily reappear and require resolution as action within the relation to the analytic other.

Because such threats to the self are linked to unmanageable experience with the other, it is only the simulation of that experience within a differently organized dyad in which the other take responsibility for their part in the experience that is therapeutic. What we strive for is not only the recovery of the story of suffering, but also the breakup of the story, once a seamless narrative of doer and done-to, in the new, therapeutic relationship. This occurs through survival, understood as the incremental transposition of the experience of retaliation and abandonment (often felt as literal repetition, for long stretches, by one or both participants) into metaphor. This metaphorical (Kristeva, 1986) capacity allows us to hold onto the reality of thoughts and feelings and own them as part of the self without insisting that they be the whole story.

How does the transposition into metaphor occur? The capacity to disidentify with any one version as the whole story and suspend identity is the very premise of the analyst's work. It is what the analysand may identify with in the analyst. Ordinarily, the analyst leaving on vacation has to be able to identify with the patient's feeling of abandonment and affirm it—"I know you feel left"—without really experiencing herself as a neglectful, abandoning bad object. Only by establishing this double position, which is of course unconsciously communicated to the analysand, can the latter feel the analyst to have survived her reproaches and truly tolerate her feeling of loss. This allows the other/analyst to become external, and to no longer be wholly identified with the persecuting, inside object. More generally, the surviving other is the one who entertains the double identification (see chapter 1), recognizing the position of the subject without wholly abandoning her own position, who is thus relieved of persecutory aspects. More and more, it has become clear, however, that this double identification has to be materialized in directed communication that allows the patient to consciously reflect on the analyst's self-expression.

As I have suggested, the analytic relationship provides some experience with the kind of intersubjective space that allows us to use identification to bridge difference, to hold multiple positions, to tolerate nonidentity rather than wipe out the position of self or other. This notion of nonidentical or doubly identified selfhood might also serve to challenge the binary principle of exclusion and inclusion, as I suggested before. Exclusion, understood in this way, means that the subject repudiates or silences the outside others who then are assimilated to the internal, dangerous abject; inclusion, conversely, allows

107

the other to become outside, to be an external being with whom identification is possible, without that identification bringing about total assimilation of self or other. Inclusion thus calls for difference, not synthesis. Politically, it cannot mean anything but the principle of sustaining continual contest and contradiction among differences, which Butler formulated, albeit from very different premises about the subject. As each different voice ascends to the position of subject of speech, however contested, it has the chance to attain the status of an outside other, rather than a repudiated abject that threatens to contaminate or reabsorb the self.

To accept this form of inclusion is a precondition of disrupting the totalizing demand to make any voice absolute, even that of the formerly excluded other, or to silence others, even the silencers. This can only mean that the self as subject can and will allow all its voices to speak, including the voice of the other within. Owning the other within diminishes the threat of the other without so that the stranger outside is no longer identical with the strange within us—not our shadow, not a shadow over us, but a separate other whose own shadow is distinguishable in the light.

References

Abelin, E. L. 1980. Triangulation, the role of the father and the origins of core gender identity during the rapprochement subphase. In *Rapprochement*, ed. R. F. Lax, S. Bach, & J. A. Burland. New York: Aronson, 151–170.

Adams, P. 1982. 'Mothering.' *m/f* 8: 40–52.

Adorno, T. W. 1966. *Negative Dialektik*. Frankfurt: Suhrkamp.

Altman, N. 1995. *The Analyst in the inner city: Race, class, and culture through a psychoanalytic lens*. Hillsdale NJ: The Analytic Press.

Appignanesi, L. & Forrester, J. 1992. *Freud's Women* New York: Basic Books.

Aron, L. 1995. The internalized primal scene. *Psychoanalytic Dialogues* 5 (2): 195–237.

———. 1996. *A Meeting of Minds: Mutuality in Psychoanalysis*. Hillsdale NJ: Analytic Press.

Bassin, D. 1997. Beyond the he and she: Postoedipal transcendence of gender polarities. *Journal of the American Psychoanalytic Association*. Special Supplement: 1997.

———. 1997. Suppl. 44: 157–190.

109

Bataille, G. 1991. Reflections on the executioner and the victim. *Yale French Studies: Literature and the Ethical Question* 79: 15–19.

Beebe, B. & Lachmann, F. 1994. Representation and internalization in infancy: Three principles of salience. *Psychoanalytic Psychology* 11: 127–165.

Belenky, M. F., Clinchy, B. M., Goldberger, N. R., & Tarule, J. M. 1986. *Women's Ways of Knowing*. New York: Basic Books.

Benhabib, S. 1992a. Feminism and the question of postmodernism. In *Situating the Self*. New York: Routledge.

———. 1992b. The Generalized and the concrete other. In *Situating the Self*. New York: Routledge.

Benhabib, S., J. Butler, N. Fraser, & D. Cornell. 1995. *Feminist Contentions*. New York & London: Routledge.

Benjamin, J. 1977. The end of internalization: Adorno's social psychology. *Telos* 32: 442–64.

———. 1986a. The Alienation of desire: Woman's masochism and ideal love. In *Woman and Psychoanalysis*, ed. J. Alpert. Hillsdale NJ: Analytic Press, 113–138.

———. 1986b. A Desire of one's own: Psychoanalytic feminism and intersubjective Space. In *Feminist Studies/Critical Studies*, ed. T. de Lauretis. Bloomington: University of Indiana Press, 78–101.

———. 1988. *The Bonds of Love*. New York: Pantheon.

———. 1991. Father and daughter: Identification with difference—a contribution to gender heterodoxy. *Psychoanalytic Dialogues* 1 (3): 277–299.

———. 1992. Reply to Schwartz. *Psychoanalytic Dialogues* 2 (3): 417–424.

———. 1995a. Recognition and destruction: An outline of intersubjectivity. In *Like Subjects, Love Objects*. New Haven: Yale University Press.

———. 1995b. Sameness and difference: An "overinclusive" view of gender constitution. In *Like Subjects, Love Objects*. New Haven: Yale University Press.

———. 1995c. The omnipotent mother: A psychoanalytic study of fantasy and reality. In *Like Subjects, Love Objects*. New Haven: Yale University Press.

Bernheimer, C. & Kahane, C. 1985. *In Dora's Case: Freud-Hysteria-Feminism*. New York: Columbia University Press.

References

Bernstein, D. 1990. Female genital anxieties, conflicts, and typical mastery modes. *International Journal of Psycho-analysis* 71: 151–165.

Bernstein, R. 1992. *The New Constellation.* Cambridge: MIT Press.

Bion, W. 1962b. *Learning from Experience.* In *Seven Servants.* New York: Aronson, 1977.

———. 1967. *Second Thoughts.* New York: Aronson.

Birksted-Breen, D. 1996. Phallus, penis and mental space. *International Journal of Psycho-analysis* 77: 649–657.

Bollas, C. 1989. *Forces of Destiny: Psychoanalysis and Human Idiom.* London: Free Association Books.

———. 1992. *On Being a Character.* New York: Hill and Wang.

Braidotti, R. 1991. *Patterns of Dissonance.* New York: Routledge.

Brennan, T. 1989. Introduction. *Between Psychoanalysis and Feminism.* London & New York: Routledge.

———. 1992. *The Interpretation of the Flesh: Freud and Femininity.* New York: Routledge.

Breuer, J. & Freud, S. 1895. *Studies in Hysteria.* In Standard Edition of the Complete Psychological Works of Sigmund Freud, Vol. 2. London: Hogarth, 1957.

Bromberg, P. M. 1993. Shadow and substance: A relational perspective on clinical process. *Psychoanalytic Psychology* 10 (2): 147–168.

———. 1995. Psychoanalysis, dissociation, and personality organization. *Psychoanalytic Dialogues* 5: 511–528.

———. 1996. Standing in the spaces: the multiplicity of self and the psychoanalytic relationship. *Contemporary Psychoanalysis* 32: 509–536.

Butler, J. 1990a. *Gender Trouble.* New York & London: Routledge.

———. 1990b. Gender trouble. In *Feminism/Postmodernism,* ed. L. Nicholson. New York: Routledge.

———. 1992. Contingent foundations: Feminism and the question of "Postmodernism." In *Feminists Theorize the Political,* eds. J. Butler and J. Scott. New York: Routledge.

———. 1993a. *Bodies That Matter.* New York: Routledge.

———. 1993b. Poststructuralism and postmarxism. *Diacritics* 23: 3–11.

———. 1995. Melancholy gender/refused identifications. *Psychoanalytic Dialogues* 5: 00.

Cascardi, A. 1992. *The Subject of Modernity*. Cambridge: Cambridge University Press.

Casement, P. J. 1991. *Learning from the Patient*. New York: Guilford Press.

Chasseguet-Smirgel, J. 1976. Freud and female sexuality. *International Journal of Psycho-analysis* 57: 275–286.

Chodorow, N. 1978. *The Reproduction of Mothering*. Berkeley: University of California Press.

———. 1980. Gender, relation and difference in psychoanalytic perspective. In *Feminism and Psychoanalytic Theory*. New Haven: Yale University Press, 1989.

———. 1985. Beyond drive theory: Object relations and the limits of radical individualism. In *Feminism and Psychoanalytic Theory*. New Haven: Yale University Press, 1989.

———. 1994. Heterosexuality as a compromise formation: reflections on the psychoanalytic theory of sexual development. *Femininities, Masculinities, Sexualities*. Lexington: University of Kentucky Press, 1994.

Christiansen, A. 1993. Masculinity and its vicissitudes. Paper presented at Seminar on Psychoanalysis and Sexual Difference, New York, New York Institute for the Humanities at New York University.

Cixous, H. & Clement, C. 1975. *La Jeune Nee*. Paris: Union Generale d'Editions, 1975.

Coates, S. 1997. Is it time to jettison the concept of developmental lines? *Gender and Psychoanalysis* 2 (1): 35–54.

Coates, S., R. Friedman, & S. Wolfe. 1991. The etiology of boyhood gender disorder. *Psychoanalytic Dialogues* 1: 481–524.

Cornell, D. 1992. *Philosophy of the Limit*. New York: Routledge.

———. 1995. Rethinking the time of feminism. In *Feminist Contentions*. New York: Routlege.

Davies, J. M. 1996. Linking the "pre-analytic" with the postclassical: Integration, dissociation, and the multiplicity of unconscious process. *Contemporary Psychyoanalysis* 32: 553–577.

Davies, J. & Frawley, M. 1994. *Treating the Adult Survivor of Sexual Abuse*. New York: Basic Books.

de Lauretis, T. 1986. Issues, terms, and contexts. In *Feminist Studies/Critical Studies*. Bloomington: University of Indiana Press, 1–19.

References

Derrida, J. 1978. Violence and metaphysics. In *Writing and Difference*, trans. A. Bass. Chicago: University of Chicago Press.

Dimen, M. 1991. Deconstructing difference: Gender, splitting, and transitional space. *Psychoanalytic Dialogues* 1 (3): 335–352.

———. 1995. The third step: Freud, the feminists, and postmodernism. *American Journal of Psychoanalysis* 55: 303–320.

Dinnerstein, D. 1976. *The Mermaid and the Minotaur*. New York: Harper & Row.

Eigen, M. 1981. The area of faith in Winnicott, Lacan, and Bion. In *The Electrified Tightrope*. Northvale NJ: Aronson, 1993.

———. 1993. *The Electrified Tightrope*. Northvale NJ: Aronson.

Fast, I. 1984. *Gender Identity*. Hillsdale NJ: The Analytic Press.

———. 1990. Aspects of early gender development: Toward a reformulation. *Psychoanalytic Psychology* 7 (supplement): 105–118.

First, E. 1988. The leaving game: I'll play you and you'll play me. The emergence of the capacity for dramatic role play in two-year-olds. In *Modes of Meaning: Clinical and Developmental Approaches to Symbolic Play*, ed. A. Slade and D. Wolfe, 132–160. New York: Oxford University Press.

Flax, J. 1990. *Thinking Fragments: Psychoanalysis, Feminism, and Postmodernism in the Contemporary West*. Berkeley: University of California Press.

Fraser, N. 1995. False antithesis: A response to Seyla Benhabib and Judith Butler. In *Feminist Contentions*. New York: Routledge.

Freedman, N. 1980. On splitting and its resolution. *Psychoanalysis and Contemporary Thought* 3, 237–66.

———. 1985. The concept of transformation in psychoanalysis. *Psychoanalytic Psychology* 2 (4): 17–39.

Freud, S. 1896. Further remarks on the neuro-psychoses of defence. Standard Edition of the Complete Psychological Works of Sigmund Freud, Vol. 3, 162–185.

———. 1900a. The Interpretation of Dreams. Standard Edition, Vol. 4. London Hogarth, 1953.

———. 1900b. Letter to Fliess, October 14. In *The Complete Letters of Sigmund Freud to Wilhelm Fliess 1887–1904*, ed. J. M. Masson, 426–27. Cambridge: Harvard University Press, 1985.

———. 1905. Fragment of an analysis of a case of hysteria. Standard Edition, Vol. 7: 3–124. London: Hogarth, 1953.

———. 1912. The dynamics of the transference. In Standard Edition, Vol. 12: 97–107. London: Hogarth.

———. 1914a. Remembering, repeating and working through. In Standard Edition, Vol. 12: 145–156. London: Hogarth Press.

———. 1914b. On narcissism: an introduction. In Standard Edition, Vol. 14: 67–102. London: Hogarth, 1957.

———. 1915a. Instincts and their vicissitudes. In Standard Edition, Vol. 14: 109–140. London: Hogarth, 1957.

———. 1915b. Observations on transference love. In Standard Edition, Vol. 12: 157–171. London: Hogarth, 1958.

———. 1917. Mourning and melancholia. In Standard Edition, Vol. 14: 237–258. London: Hogarth Press, 1957.

———. 1920. The Psychogenesis of a Case of Homosexuality in a Woman. Standard Edition, Vol. 18: 145–172. London: Hogarth, 1955.

———. 1921. Group psychology and the analysis of the ego. In Standard Edition, Vol. 18: 67–144. London: Hogarth Press, 1955.

———. 1923. The Ego and the id. In Standard Edition, Vol. 19: 1–66. London: Hogarth, 1961.

———. 1925. Some psychical consequences of the anatomical distinction between the sexes. In Standard Edition, Vol. 19: 248–260. London: Hogarth, 1961.

———. 1930. Civilization and its discontents. In Standard Edition, Vol. 21: 59–197. London: Hogarth, 1953.

———. 1931. Female sexuality. Standard Edition Vol. 21: 225–246. London: Hogarth, 1961.

———. 1933. New introductory lectures on psychoanalysis: Femininity. Standard Edition, Vol. 22: 112–135. London: Hogarth, 1961.

Fuss, D. 1989. *Essentially Speaking: Feminism, Nature and Difference*. New York: Routledge.

Gallop, J. 1982. *The Daughter's Seduction: Feminism and Psychoanalysis*. Ithaca, NY: Cornell University Press.

———. 1988. Penis/phallus: same difference. In *Thinking Through the Body*. New York: Columbia University Press.

Gabbard, G. 1995. Contertransference: The emerging common ground. *International Journal of Psychoanalysis* 76: 475–486.

References

Gerson, S. 1996a. Neutrality, resistance, and self-disclosure in an intersubjective psychoanalysis. *Psychoanalytic Dialogues* 6: 623–645.

———. 1996b. A shared body of language. *Gender and Psychoanalysis* 1: 345–360.

Gill, M. 1994. *Psychoanalysis in Transition*. Hillsdale NJ: Analytic Press.

Gilligan, C. 1982. *In a Different Voice*. Cambridge: Harvard University Press.

Goldner, V. 1991. Toward a critical relational theory of gender. *Psychoanalytic Dialogues* 1 (3): 249–272.

Green, A. 1986. *On Private Madness*. Madison CT: International Universities Press.

Greenberg, J. 1996. Psychoanalytic words and psychoanalytic acts: A brief history. *Contemporary Psychoanalysis* 32 (2): 177–184.

Greenson, R. 1968. Dis-identifying from mother: its special importance for the boy. *International Journal of Psycho-analysis* 49: 370–374.

Habermas, J. 1992. Individuation through socialization: George Herbert Meade's theory of subjectivity," in *Postmetaphysical Thinking*, trans. W. Hohengarten. Cambridge: MIT Press.

Harraway, D. 1985. A manifesto for cyborgs. *Socialist Review* 15 (2): 65–107.

Harris, A. 1991. Gender as contradiction: A discussion of Freud's "The psychogenesis of a case of homosexuality in a woman." *Psychoanalytic Dialogues* 1 (2): 197–224.

Hillman, U. 1992. Bertha Pappenheim: Psychoanalyse—Frauenbewegung—Sozialarbeit. In *FrauenStadtbuch Frankfurt*, WEIBH.

Hoffman, I. 1991. Reply to Benjamin. *Psychoanalytic Dialogues* 1 (4): 535–544.

Hoffman, L. 1996. Freud and women's subjectivity. Paper delivered at the New York Psychoanalytic Institute, February 1996.

Horney, K. 1924. On the genesis of the castration complex in women. In *Feminine Psychology*. New York: Norton, 1967.

———. 1926. The flight from womanhood. In *Feminine Psychology*. New York: Norton, 1967.

Irigaray, L. 1985. *Speculum of the Other Woman*. Ithaca, NY: Cornell University Press.

———. 1991. The bodily encounter with the mother. In *The Irigary reader*, ed. M. Whirford, 34–46. Oxford: Basil Blackwell.

Kerr, J. 1993. *A Most Dangerous Method: The Story of Jung, Freud and Sabina Spielrein*. New York, Random House.

Klein, M. 1928. Early stages of the Oedipus conflict. In *Contributions to Psychoanalysis*. New York: McGraw Hill, 1964.

———. 1946. Notes on some schizoid mechanisms. In *Contributions to Psychoanalysis*. New York: McGraw Hill, 1964.

Kohlberg, L. 1981. *The Philosophy of Moral Development*. San Francisco: Harper and Row.

Kohut, H. 1977. *The Restoration of the Self*. New York: International Universities Press.

Kojeve, A. 1969. *Introduction to the Reading of Hegel*. New York: Basic Books.

Kris, A. 1994. Freud's treatment of a narcissistic patient. *International Journal of Psychoanalysis* 75: 649–664.

Kristeva, J. 1982. *Powers of Horror: An Essay on Abjection*. New York: Columbia University Press.

———. 1986. Freud and Love. In *Tales of Love*. New York: Columbia University Press.

Lacan, J. 1977a. The mirror stage as formative of the function of the I. In *Ecrits: A Selection*, trans. A. Sheridan. New York: Norton.

———. 1977b. The signification of the phallus. In *Ecrits: A Selection*, trans. A. Sheridan. New York: Norton.

———. 1988. *The Seminar of Jacques Lacan: Book I, Frued's Papers on Technique; Book II, The Ego in Freud's Theory*. New York: Norton.

Lesser, R. 1997. A plea for throwing development out with the bathwater: Commentary on Benjamin's "In Defense of Gender Ambiguity." *Gender and Psychoanalysis* 2. In press.

Lewes, K. 1988. *The Psychoanalytic Theory of Male Homosexuality*. New York: Simon & Schuster.

Loewald, H. 1976. The waning of the oedipus complex. In *Papers on Psychoanalysis*. New Haven: Yale University Press.

Mahler, M., Pine, F., & Bergmann, A. 1975. *The Psychological Birth of the Human Infant*. New York: Basic Books.

Mahoney, M. & Yngvesson, B. 1992. The Construction of subjectivity and the paradox of resistance: Reintegrating feminist anthropology & psychology. *Signs* 18: 44–73.

References

Maroda, K. 1995. Projective identification and counter-transference interventions: since feeling is first. *Psychoanalytic Review* 82: 229–248.

Martin, B. 1982. Feminism, criticism, and Foucault. *New German Critique* 27: 3–30.

May, R. 1986. Concerning a psychoanalytic view of maleness. *Psychoanalytic Review* 73: 175–193.

Mayer, E. 1985. Everybody must be like me. *International Journal of Psychoanalysis* 66: 331–348.

McDougall, J. 1986a. Eve's reflections: On the homosexual components of female sexuality. In H. Meyers ed. *Between Analyst and Patient*. New York: Analytic Press.

Menaker, E. 1942. The Masochistic factor in the psychoanalytic situation. In *Masochism and the Emergent Ego* Northvale, NJ: Aronson, 1996.

Meyers, D. 1994. *Subjection & Subjectivity*. New York: Routledge.

Mitchell, J. 1974. *Psychoanalysis and Feminism*. New York: Pantheon.

———. 1982. Introduction 1 to *Feminine Sexuality: Jacques Lacan and the Ecole Freudienne*, eds. J. Mitchell and J. Rose. New York: Norton.

———. 1991. Commentary on "Deconstructing difference: gender, splitting, and transitional space." *Psychoanalytic Dialogues* 1: 353–359.

———. 1995. Unpublished Colloquium. New York University, January 1995.

Mitchell, S. 1993. *Hope and Dread in Psychoanalysis*. New York: Basic Books.

———. 1996. Gender and sexual orientation in the age of postmodernism: the plight of the perplexed clinician. *Gender and Psychoanalysis* 1: 45–73.

Moi, T. 1985a. Representation of patriarchy: Sexuality and epistemology in Freud's Dora. In *In Dora's Case: Freud-Hysteria-Feminism*, eds. Bernheimer & Kahane. New York: Columbia University Press.

———. 1985b. *Sexual/Textual Politics*. London: Methuen.

Nicholson, L. 1990. *Feminism/Postmodernism*. New York: Routledge.

Ogden, T. 1986. *The Matrix of the Mind*. Northvale NJ: Aronson.

———. 1987. The transitional oedipal relationship in female development. *International Journal of Psycho-analysis* 68: 485–498.

———. 1994. *Subjects of Analysis*. Northvale NJ: Aronson.

O'Connor, N. & Ryan, J. 1993. *Wild Desires and Mistaken Identities*. New York: Columbia University Press.

Pappenheim, B. 1912. Die Frau im kirchlichen und religiosen leben. In Wagner, L., Mehrwald, S., Maierhof, G., Jansen, M. 1994 *Aus Dem Leben Judischer Frauen.* Kassel: Archiv der Deutschen Frauenbewegung.

Person, E. S. & Ovesey, L. 1983. Psychoanalytic theories of gender identity. *Journal of the American Academy of Psychoanalysis* 11: 203–226.

Pizer, S. 1992. The negotiation of paradox in the analytic process. *Psychoanalytic Dialogues* 2: 215–240.

———. 1996. The distributed self: Introduction to Symposium on "The Multiplicity of Self and Analytic Technique." *Contemporary Psychoanalysis* 32: 499–508.

Racker, H. 1968. *Transference and Countertransference.* London: Maresfield Library, Karnac, 1982.

Renik, O. 1996. The perils of neutrality. *Psychoanalytic Quarterly* 65: 495–517.

Rivera, M. 1989. Linking the psychological and the social: Feminism, poststructuralism and multiple personality. *Dissociation* 2: 24–31.

Rose, J. 1982. Introduction 2 to *Feminine Sexuality: Jacques Lacan and the Ecole Freudienne,* eds. J. Mitchell and J. Rose. New York: Norton.

———. 1985. Dora: Fragment of an analysis. In *In Dora's Case: Freud-Hysteria-Feminism,* eds. Bernheimer & Kahane. New York: Columbia University Press.

———. 1986. *Sexuality in the Field of Vision.* London: Verso.

Rosenfeld, H. 1971. Contribution to the psychopathology of psychotic states: The importance of projective identification in the ego structure and the object relations of the psychotic patient. In *Melanie Klein Today,* Vol 1, ed. E. Spillius. London: Routledge, 1988.

Rubin, G. 1975. The traffic in women: Notes on the political economy of sex. In R. Reiter (ed.) *Toward an Anthropology of Women.* New York: Monthly Review Press.

Ruddick, S. 1989. *Maternal Thinking.* Boston: Beacon.

Sandler, J. 1993. On communication from patient to analyst: Not everything is projective identification. *International Journal of Psychoanalysis* 74 (6): 1097–1108.

Santner, E. 1996. *My Own Private Germany: Daniel Paul Schreber's Secret History of Modernity.* Princeton: Princeton Press.

Schwartz, H. 1994. From dissociation to negotiation: A relational psychoanalytic perspective on multiple personality disorder. *Psychoanalytic Psychology* 11 (2): 189–233.

References

Scott, J. 1993. The tip of the volcano. *Society for Comparative Study of Society and History*, 438–451.

Segal, H. 1957. Notes on symbol formation. *International Journal of Psychoanalysis* 38: 391–397.

Shapiro, S. 1996. The embodied analyst in the Victorian consulting room. *Gender and Psychoanalysis* 1 (3): 297–322.

Showalter, E. 1985. *The Female Malady: Women, Madness and English Culture, 1893–1980*. New York: Penguin.

Silverman, D. 1987. What are little girls made of? *Psychoanalytic Psychology* 4: 315–334.

Simons, M. & Benjamin, J. 1997. Simone de Beauvoir: An interview. *Feminist Studies* 5: 332–345.

Simons, M. (in press) *Feminism, Race, and the Origins of Existentialism: Beauvoir's Second Sex*.

Skolnick, N. & Warshaw, S. eds. 1992. *Relational Perspectives in Psychoanalysis*. Hillsdale NJ: The Analytic Press.

Smith, P. 1988. *Discerning the Subject*. Minneapolis: University of Minnesota Press.

Spezzano, C. 1993. *Affect in Psychoanalysis: A Clinical Synthesis*. Hillsdale NJ: The Analytic Press.

————. 1996a. The three faces of two-person psychology: Development, ontology, and epistemology. *Psychoanalytic Dialogues* 6: 599–622.

————. 1996b. Fusions and ruptures: Responses to Cooper's further remarks. *Psychanalytic Dialogues* 6: 909–916.

Sprengnether, M. 1990. *The Spectral Mother: Freud, feminism, and psychoanalysis*. Ithaca NY: Cornell University Press.

————. 1995. Reading Freud's life. *American Imago* 52: 9–54.

Stern, D. 1985. *The Interpersonal World of the Infant*. New York: Basic Books.

Stern, D. B. 1992. Commentary on constructivism in clinical psychoanalysis *Psychoanalytic Dialogues* 2: 331–363.

Stoller, R. J. 1968. *Sex and Gender*. New York: Aronson.

————. 1973. Facts and fancies: An examination of Freud's concept of bisexuality. In *Women and Analysis*, ed. J. Strouse, 340–363. Boston: G. K. Hall.

Stolorow, R. & Atwood, G. 1984. *Structures of Subjectivity: Explorations in psychoanalytic phenomenology*. Hillsdale NJ: The Analytic Press.

Stolorow, R., Brandschaft, B., & Atwood, G. 1987. *Psychoanalytic Treatment: An Intersubjective Approach*. Hillsdale NJ: The Analytic Press.

Target, M. & Fonagy, P. 1996. Playing with Reality: II. The development of psychic reality from a theoretical perspective. *International Journal of Psycho-analysis* 77: 459–479.

Theweleit, K. 1987. *Male Fantasies*, Vols. 1 and 2, trans. Stephen Conway. Minneapolis: University of Minnesota Press.

Tronick, E. 1989. Emotions and Emotional Communication. *American Psychology* 44: 112–119.

Weir, A. 1996. *Sacrificial Logics: Feminist Theory and the Critique of Identity*. New York: Routledge.

Whitebook, J. 1994. Hypostatizing Thanatos: Lacan's analysis of the ego. *Constellations* 1 (2): 214–230.

Winnicott, D. W. 1971. The use of an object and relating through identifications. In *Playing and Reality*. London: Tavistock.

Young, I. M. 1990. The ideal of community and the politics of difference. In *Feminism/Postmodernism*, ed. L. Nicholson, 300–323. New York: Routledge.

Zizek, S. 1991. *Looking Awry: An Introduction to Jacques Lacan Through Popular Culture*. Cambridge: MIT Press.

———. 1995. Unpublished Colloquium, Columbia University.

Index

Philosophy of the Limit (Cornell), 103
Pinel, ___., 6
postmodernism, feminist position in, 37, 80, 82–83, 85, 92
postoedipal
  complementarity, 34, 59
  as development term, 70
  symbolism of, 72
poststructuralism, 83
pregenital polymorphism, 74
Preliminary Communication (Freud, 1893), 12
preoedipal formation
  in boys, 46
  in women, 44, 45, 47, 55
preoedipal inclusivity, oedipal complementarity and, 58–69
primal leap (*Ursprung*), of psychoanalysis, 1–34
psychoanalysis
  evolution of, 10
  feminist theory and, xii, xiii, xv
  intersubjective view of, xv, xx
  primal leap (*Ursprung*) of, 1–34
  recognition in, xiii

R

Racker, Heinrich, 19
Rank, Otto, 14
reason, Freud on, 14, 15, 16
reciprocity, 100
recognition
  as activity, 29
  in feminist theory, xviii, 100
  intersubjective conception of, 29
  metaphor of, 27
  in psychoanalysis, xiii
recognition/negation, 96
  subordination alternation with, 97
Reich, Wilhelm, 2
reification process, 54–55, 75
relational analysts, 46–47
relational self, of women, 36
"Remembering, Repeating and Working Through" (Freud), 13
resistance
  of Dora, 16
  of patient, 12–13
reversal, of complementarity against mother, 30
Rivera, Margo, 106
Riviere, Joan, 21, 22
Rose, Jacqueline, 48, 52
Rubin, Gail, 50

S

sadism, 98
sadomasochism, xii
  Freud on, 40
Salpetrière, 6
Samuels, Andrew, 71
Sartre, Jean-Paul, xi
Schiller, Friedrich, 14
"The Second Sex—Thirty Years Later" [conference, 1979], xi
see-saw relationships, xiv, xv
the self
  identification and, 79
  intersubjective theory of, 80
  knowledge of, 100
  splitting of, 88–89, 97–98, 99, 102, 105
self-other, dialogue of, xix, xv, 106

Made in the USA
Coppell, TX
22 October 2020